M000195956

Eph. 5:33

THE BEST
MARRIAGE EVER

God's Guide to a Masterful Matrimony

THE BEST

MARRIAGE EVER

Donnie Van Curen

TATE PUBLISHING
AND **ENTERPRISES**, LLC

The Best Marriage Ever
Copyright © 2012 by Donnie Van Curen All rights reserved.

No part of this publication may be reproduced, stored in a retrieval system or transmitted in any way by any means, electronic, mechanical, photocopy, recording or otherwise without the prior permission of the author except as provided by USA copyright law.

Scripture quotations taken from the *New American Standard Bible®*, Copyright © 1960, 1962, 1963, 1968, 1971, 1972, 1973, 1975, 1977, 1995 by The Lockman Foundation. Used by permission.

The opinions expressed by the author are not necessarily those of Tate Publishing, LLC.

Published by Tate Publishing & Enterprises, LLC
127 E. Trade Center Terrace | Mustang, Oklahoma 73064 USA
1.888.361.9473 | www.tatepublishing.com

Tate Publishing is committed to excellence in the publishing industry. The company reflects the philosophy established by the founders, based on Psalm 68:11,
"The Lord gave the word and great was the company of those who published it."

Book design copyright © 2012 by Tate Publishing, LLC. All rights reserved.
Cover design by Allen Jomoc
Interior design by Ronnel L. Luspoc

Published in the United States of America

ISBN: 978-1-62147-323-7

1. Religion / Christian Life / Love & Marriage
2. Family & Relationships / Marriage
12.09.18

Dedication

This book is dedicated to my Lord and Savior and is a product of the love, sacrifice, and commitment of my incredible family.

Thank you, Heather, for being all I could imagine or wish for in a wife and partner. You are an amazing spouse and a wonderful mom. I look forward to many more years of sharing our life together.

Thank you, Madison and Christian, you both make me extremely proud and blessed to be a father. I pray that someday the words in this book will guide each of you to a happy and healthy relationship of your own.

I love each of you with all my heart and forever.

—Love, a loving husband and father

Contents

Dedication   5

Introduction   9

What Marriage Is and Isn't   15

Building Your Wall:
Two Stronger Than One   35

Keys to Success   49

Communication: Learn To Speak French   69

Expectations: For Better and For Worse   87

Differences: His Needs, Her Needs   109

Perception is Reality   127

Conflict:
A Necessary Evil or Not?   145

A Few Words about Sex   159

Divorce and Blended Families   171

Introduction

When I made the decision back in 2006 to pursue a career in counseling, it was never my intention to write a book. Until recently, my writing experience consisted of birthday cards and an occasional letter to friends or family members. I don't believe I fully realized what an impact the written word could have until my wife's illness in 2011. At the end of January 2011, Heather contracted a serious life threatening condition called Sepsis. What we thought was the flu, in three short days, would leave her in a sedated state on a ventilator struggling to live. Heather would eventually spend thirteen days in the ICU and another fourteen days in the hospital. It is amazing how quickly life can change. One day I was packing for a trip to Pebble Beach with my brother and dad, and the next day I was in a waiting room with over fifty people praying that my wife would live.

I can say with certainty that this experience changed my life. Never have I been in a situation where I felt so lost and so *not* in control. This was a foreign concept for me. All my life I have desired control. In my career, in my relationships, even with my children, control was something to be sought after, something to be attained. Yet this was taken from me in such a quick and unexpected way, it was hard to get any real perspective. Each day in the ICU felt like forever. I spent many nights on the floor of the waiting room praying that

God would heal the wife I missed so much. I recall how much I missed her voice, her smile, and those beautiful brown eyes. During the first week of Heather's illness, my family arrived for support. I believe at one point, we had sixteen people staying at the house. To some this may sound crazy, and many of my friends worried that this was too many people. Truth be known, it was exactly what the kids and I needed. The support we received from my family that first week was nothing short of miraculous. It was like water to a thirsty man. Each person played their own specific role, working tirelessly to support and love me and my family.

It was at this time that my sister-in-law found the site CaringBridge.org. In my wildest dreams, I could not have imagined that so many people would reach out to us and our family during our time of need. We were receiving so many calls and prayers from people all over the country that it was hard to keep up. My family thought a universal site would be a great way to reach people and give people the ability to reach us. How right they were. We posted the first message on February 2, and from that point on, it was my lifeline. Each day was an opportunity to post my thoughts and feelings, often more than once. This site became my journal, and the entire world was able to read it. It was also a source of tremendous encouragement, as people across the United States left messages of encouragement and support for our entire family.

I would write when I was happy, and I would write when I was sad. My writing would take on whatever mood I was in at the time. What God was doing in my life would manifest itself into my writings. I found that people would respond to almost each and every entry. It was as if God was working through me to touch others and at the same time working through others to touch me. I recall a conversation with a dear friend many weeks after Heather left the hospital. He had been reading my post and wanted to know how I remained so strong during such a time of difficulty. I thought about his question for a minute. The last thing I was feeling in those moments was strength. I was surprised that anyone could have seen anything short of weakness from my fear and anguish. I realized, and later told my friend, that any strength exhibited in my writings was what God was providing me at the time. I was weak, but He was strong. God granted me a wonderful opportunity to offer transparency during our ordeal. For many months after leaving the hospital, Heather and I heard repeated stories of God's work on other's lives through her illness. What an amazing privilege to experience God in such a way.

Not long after Heather left the ICU, I joined my friend Jerry Roberts for lunch at a local Asian restaurant. Jerry had been my rock and encouragement through Heather's illness. He and his wife, Sherry, were our prayer warriors, among many others, and their friendship is a daily blessing. At the end of our lunch, we received fortune cookies. I opened mine to read the following message, "You have a charming way with words and should write a book." I laughed at the thought but had recently heard this from many people reading the CaringBridge site. When I returned to the hospital, Heather had just finished a visit with several ladies that had communicated the same message. I am not one to get in the way of God's plans, and as a result of obedience and my pure desire to see marriages changed by His hands, you have the existence of this book.

The title of this book is a product of my wonderful son Christian's passion for life. During a particular stage in his life, everything was described as the "best ever." I was the "best dad ever," his mom was the "best mom ever," our vacation that summer was the "best vacation ever," hamburgers eaten during this time were the "best ever," and even Dr. Pepper was the "best drink ever" (no argument here). Now this isn't to say that Christian had not tasted better drinks, had better vacations, or even found a better burger, but it was more of an expression of passion. The title of this book and its contents are about my passion for marriage.

There is nothing more important to me, or my world, than God and His wonderful impact on the institution of marriage. I have had a very strong opinion of marriage ever since my parents' divorce, when I was only eight years of age. God blessed my life despite this event, and he also gave to me a passion for this lifelong commitment. I believe a strong marriage is a result of two people committed to one another with God as their foundation. A strong marriage has a lasting effect on money, careers, children, friendships, and life. Doing it right, makes a difference. I know because my marriage is still a work in progress. I, not unlike Paul in Philippians 3, "do not regard myself as having laid hold" of a perfect marriage relationship, "but I press on toward the goal for the prize of the upward call of God in Christ Jesus," which is a marriage committed to His glory and will. With twenty years of marriage under my belt, I can say with certainty that I have everything I could have dreamed of in a wife and in a relationship. However, I also know that it is a journey with no end. The enemy would like nothing more than to destroy the relationship I have with Heather, and he will do everything in his power to try and destroy what God has brought together. But I remain alert and aware of each attack, equipping me and my marriage to overcome any and all obstacles for God's glory and honor. This book is dedicated to everyone in the same battle.

I have written this book for couples engaged or married. You will even find a chapter for those dealing with blended families. Regardless of your age or number of marriages, if you want to improve the relationship you have with the one you love, this book is for you. There are many principles and stories throughout the following pages that will entertain and educate you, feel free to skip around. This book is intended to be an opportunity for me to share my passion with you, in hopes that God will reveal Himself through each page. The order is not as important as the content. However, there is a flow to each chapter and you may find it more beneficial to go in order. As a couple, read the book separately or read it together, but make sure you are discussing the content and growing together. I have included couple application questions at the end of each chapter. I would highly recommend doing these together with your spouse. May God equip you and yours to fully recognize and enjoy what only He can provide: *the greatest marriage ever.*

What Marriage Is and Isn't

It is December 19, 1992. I am a young twenty-three-year-old college graduate getting ready to marry my beautiful young fiancée. We had known each other since the fall of 1988, when I had poured a pitcher of beer over her head at a fraternity party. We started dating in the summer of 1991. Why such a long period of time between our introduction and dating? You might say a college degree made me smarter and, thus, a better judge of women, and as a result, I pursued a relationship with this beautiful brown-eyed, Stillwater, Oklahoma, native and would not take no for an answer. Truth be told, when I approached Heather to take our relationship to another level, she was dating someone else. It took several dates and many yellow roses to convince her that I was the man of her dreams, as I knew she was the woman of mine.

As I waited in my black tux for my bride to walk down the aisle, I couldn't help but dream of what was to come. We had our whole life ahead of us and felt we had a great start on a wonderful relationship. That winter day we said our vows, ate some cake, drank some punch, and were married—pretty simple stuff. Marriages happen every day around the globe similar to ours, but somehow, somewhere, something goes wrong. Do we fully understand what marriage is? Do we, as a society, fully appreciate the covenant that exists between a man and a woman? Do we also fully appreciate God's role and place within this sacred union? I know I didn't.

Under God

Genesis 1:27 says, "God created man in His own image, in the image of God He created him; male and female He created them." Both men and women were created by God and for Him. God desired fellowship, and thus, He created man. Our marriage should make fellowship with God a priority. A marriage without God is like driving without directions. There is no doubt you are going somewhere, but where? About the time couples enter my office with difficulties in their relationship is about that time they recognize that the direction they are going is not the right one. We often want to believe that once we say our vows and exchange rings, we have a marriage. But the truth is that only God can create a true union. With Him, a couple has unlimited opportunities to grow in Christ and within their relationship. Without Him we are forced to set priorities and expectations that lead us down a road unintended and without promise. I am not saying that there are not good marriages outside of a relationship with Christ. But if you want a great marriage, shouldn't you start with the Creator of the actual institution? Several years ago, I was vacationing in Colorado with my family and had the opportunity to fly-fish for the first time. During our trip, I spent an entire day with a wonderful guide catching somewhere around twenty trout in the streams surrounding Crested Butte, Colorado. Later in the week, I decided to go back to the streams my guide had taken me to and try it alone. In no less than one hour, I had lost three flies, cut up at least two feet of line, and I hadn't even been in the water yet! Needless to say, I found out how truly valuable my guide was. Marriage does not have to be difficult, but you must have a guide. God and His Word are the only guide you will need for a meaningful and productive relationship.

Yet, even when couples have God in their relationship, they still struggle. The divorce rate of Christians involved in church is very similar to that of those outside of the church. How is it that people who have the answer seldom apply it? I have to wonder if they even know they have the answer. Even within Christian relationships, God can be absent. Ecclesiastes 4:12 says, "And if one can overpower him who is alone, two can resist him. A cord of three stands is not quickly torn apart." The strength, purpose, and prosperity of relationships come not from two individuals but three. Many times in my own marriage, Heather and I have not had the answers. From job offers, finding a church home, difficulties with family, to conflict with our kids, together we are strong, but many times that is not enough. We need a third person to make the difference, and this person in our marriage is God. Let me offer an example.

Recently our family has struggled with finding a church home. We had served one place for over ten years, but both Heather and I felt the Lord calling us away. Over a six-month period, we visited several different churches and denominations praying for God's direction, talking about what God was communicating to our family after each visit. Heather and I had differing opinions on where to serve, but we were both open to God's calling and obedience to Him. One evening at dinner Madison, my daughter, commented that since every church we visited had something our family was not comfortable with, maybe God was calling us back to our home church. This had been on my mind for some time, and it was something Heather had considered as well, but to have it come from our fourteen-year-old daughter was an awesome act of God working through our family. That night we recognized God's answer to our prayers and immediately went back to our home church. I do not know why God called us away only to send us back. All I do know is that He had called us back, and, therefore, we obeyed. God did not design life to be lived alone; He designed it to show our need for Him. We are at our best when we put God at the center of our world. He knows what we need, He knows what will fulfill our deepest desires, and He wants to reveal Himself to you and me every day. God's presence in a marriage makes the difference. In Philippians 4:19, Paul writes, "And my God will supply all your needs according to His riches in glory in Christ Jesus." This also covers our needs as couples. Forgetting God in a relationship turns a cord of three strands into two. I wonder when two will not be strong enough?

Now that we are clear that marriage is as much of a relationship with God as it is a relationship between two people, let's look at some common misconceptions people can have about the actual marriage relationship.

Two Become One

First, marriage is not two individuals but one couple. We enter a relationship from an individual perspective, and it is normal to have conflict because of our wants and needs compared to that of our spouse. But at some point, a couple must start thinking like a couple and let the power of two take effect. I live in Oklahoma and have spent a large portion of my life here, where football is king. Like it or hate it, football has always and will always be the passion of this state. In football there are many different coaches and coordinators regardless of the skill level. For general purposes there is an offensive coordinator and defensive coordinator. Both have a specific role in the game plan and ultimate success of a team, but both also have unique roles, responsibilities, and talents. In order to be successful, both coaches must be at their best together. Without collaboration of effort, you can have dysfunction and ultimate defeat, regardless of talent. Marriage is two talents playing together for the same goal. If one focuses too much on themselves, the other will be neglected, and the team suffers. Both must be aware of the other and willing to work together for the optimum outcome. This is one of the reasons I try to steer newlyweds away from separate bank accounts. Not that there is anything wrong with separating bills and money within a relationship, but the opportunity for a couple to make decisions together and to grow intimately is limited when two people live any aspect that effects both parties separately.

Many times a week, couples enter my office in crisis

caused by hot buttons or subjects that create intense anxiety, bitterness, and anger. Any time these subjects present themselves, chaos ensues. It can be over money, sex, children, work, in-laws, or even politics. When we explore these hot buttons in session, it becomes very evident that the issues in question are being seen from a purely individual point of view. Both spouses are so concerned about their position on the subject that they seldom take the time to consider the other persons' position or its impact on the relationship. In other words, the subject is more important than the relationship. Truth be told, very often the subject has nothing to do with the relationship, with exception of the position both spouses allow it to play. A very good example of this may be Heather's and my first argument as a married couple. It was in February of 1993. We had only been married a few short months, and I wanted to surprise Heather with a short two-day cruise out of Tampa for Valentine's Day. We were living in a two-bedroom apartment, starting the process of living together and learning about each other. During this time Heather was concerned about our apartment and wanted to do all she could to make it a home. One of her areas of focus was drapes. Heather felt like drapes would brighten up the apartment. I, on the other hand, felt like they were a waste of money and blinds were sufficient. This was very much a male versus female conversation. At some point not long after our discussion on the drapes, I surprised Heather with the news about our cruise and Valentine's Day but didn't quite get the response I was looking for. It upset her that I could go out and spend hundreds of dollars on a cruise, but she could not spend less money on drapes. It didn't matter that the cruise was for the both of us (my argument), what hurt her was the lack of discussion and feelings of being insignificant within our relationship. We would eventually work things out but not without a lot of tears, emotions, and, at times, cross words. What I had not learned yet as a young husband is that neither issue was more important than the relationship. My role as a husband was to understand Heather's point of view and to share mine in a way that allowed us to stay close and connected, not to drift apart. If our thoughts can stay focused on the relationship and avoid an individual point of view, we can more effectively maneuver the land mines of life and stay strong when others might not. This also allows both couples to feel safe within the relationship and thus free to communicate to the other regardless of the subject matter.

Complete

A second misconception as related to the marriage relationship is that by joining your life to another, you will be complete. But the real story is that only God can complete you. Let me explain this from another direction. I have found that people do not want to be alone. Alone is often associated with failure and misery. Online dating services and matchmakers have turned this into a very profitable business. In 2008 the online dating business had revenues of $957 million dollars in the United States alone. These revenues are expected to increase by 10 percent by 2013[1]. This is a very real illustration of the need people have to find a companion, a soul mate, a partner. Yet despite this desire, the numbers continue to remain stable for divorce in our country, somewhere around 50 percent, and the divorce rate is even higher for second and third marriages. It's as if we believe that marriage will meet some deep-hearted need and maybe make us the person we want to be or, at minimum, make life a little better. But regardless of the person you are when you get married, you will still be that person after the wedding. You will have the same insecurities, the same fears, the same personality, the same parents, the same intellect, the same emotions, and even the same temper.

My younger sister, Christie, once told me that her desire and goal was to have a marriage like mine. Now at first glance, this statement made me very proud. It was further affirmation of Heather's and my commitment to marriage and to each other. It was extremely fulfilling to think that others see a difference in our marriage, a uniqueness that is desired and valued. But what I wanted Christie to know was that the difference in our marriage is God and our commitment to Him. There is nothing magical about Heather or myself. We do not possess any special powers or talents that allow us a marriage without challenges or difficulties. But we do possess the desire to love each other out of obedience to God, not obligation to each other. If my love for Heather was based on her ability to meet my needs or satisfy my desires, it would never last. This goes for Heather's love for me as well. We are both human, and regardless of our desires or the intent of our hearts, we will eventually fail each other. This has been our destiny since Adam and Eve. However, if I focus my love on the Father, He never fails. My satisfaction and peace comes from this relationship, not from my marriage. But through my relationship with the Father I am able to love Heather unconditionally. I do not replace what she needs from God; I only enhance what God provides within her life. Completeness does not come from a person but a relationship, and that relationship is with our God and Lord Jesus Christ. John 10:10 says, "I came that they may have life, and have it more abundantly." Without Christ in your heart and a daily relationship with Him in your life, true abundance will be lacking. This is the road to completeness, and your life—and marriage—will never be the same.

Problems

A third misconception I see in marriages today is that by marrying that special someone, the problems I have with myself mystically disappear. The problem with this concept is the lack of change. Addition is not subtraction. Adding someone into your life does not subtract your specific issues. As a matter of fact, it often magnifies them. So many people today get married over and over again, trying to find Mr. or Mrs. Right, only to miss the fact that the problem in all these relationships may have been looking at them in the mirror all along.

Let me give you an example. I had the opportunity a few years back of spending time with a young couple preparing to marry. He was several years younger than she, and the conflict that this created showed up in several of our sessions. Regardless of this young man's age, he would still need respect and the opportunity to lead within the relationship. Without this respect, difficulties would soon follow. The problem existed primarily because of this young lady's upbringing. You see, she had lost her mother at a young age and had taken the responsibility of caring for both her father and brother throughout most of her high school years. This created a very strong, controlling, take-charge woman. These are great attributes for any marriage—but within reason. Control became a comfort for her as she sought to avoid tragedy like she had experienced from her mother's death. Many times control, whether real or make believe, still is a source of comfort. After they married, she would find herself more aggressive and commanding, which would cause her new husband to retreat and become distant. Eventually, she worried about an affair. As I recently worked with this couple, it became evident that the husband's ability to lead and connect with his wife was conditioned by the wife's willingness to give up control. This would only come by letting go of her need for control and embracing her fears, present before she met her husband.

Like this couple and many others, we all bring baggage into our relationships. Yet a relationship by itself is not conditioned to confront or embrace all these issues. Your spouse didn't marry you to fix you any more than you married your spouse to fix them. Our ability to grow and embrace the many problems in our individual lives comes from growth and maturity, along with God's power to do a work in us. When individuals stop growing, so do relationships. A marriage is like a body; you are only as strong as your weakest part. As a hobby I like to compete in triathlons. The race I am currently training for is a 1.25-mile swim, followed by a 60-mile ride, ending with a 13-mile run. Swimming is the easiest event for me, and I find it takes little training. In most events I have little difficulty being in the top third of all the participants in the swimming segment. The problem is that I am always in the bottom third in the run. My overall time and ability to be successful in these events is conditioned on my ability to successfully compete in all three events, not just swimming. A strong swim will never overcome a weak run. In marriage you need to both be strong and growing stronger. Genesis 2:23 says, "The man said this is now bone of my bones, and flesh of my flesh; She shall be called woman, because she was taken out of man." In other words, we are one. As Heather grows so do I; as I grow so does Heather. Growth in our marriage didn't come because of a ceremony; it came because we both addressed the areas in each of us that needed to grow.

Cohabitation

A fourth misconception I would like to address is the area of cohabitation or living together. Marriage is not cohabitation. Living together does not require the same commitment that marriage requires. In our society today, people have become comfortable with cohabitation as a precursor to marriage. But studies do not support any greater success in marriage coming from living together. The first problem with cohabitation is that it makes it somewhat easy to exit the relationship. Both parties know this, and it has an impact on the relationship. When you know you or your partner can leave at the drop of a hat, conflict is often approached differently. When you marry, more is involved in separating, and this affects the pressures that exist when conflict arrives. Secondly, don't underestimate the impact others' opinions have on your relationship. It's one thing to be living together but very much another to be husband and wife. People see you and acknowledge you as a couple when you are married. They treat you more as a unit and less as two individuals. Family is more involved and plays a different role from cohabitation to marriage. The bottom line is that marriage cannot be effectively duplicated by living together. The pressures and commitments are entirely different. Making a marriage work only happens when two people commit to making it work within the bond of a marital commitment.

The Fairy Tale

The fifth misconception is that marriage is, can, or should be a fairy tale. Regardless of your personality and that of your mate's, you will face obstacles and adversity as a married couple. This isn't a prediction; this is a promise. My late pastor, Alan Day, once said, "You are either coming out of a crisis, in between crisis, or entering crisis." Difficult times have nothing to do with people or relationships—it is a product of life. Some couples, when facing adversity in their marriage for the first time, may start to doubt the relationship or choice of partner. But a better approach is to recognize the opportunities that exist to conquer the challenges of life together. Strength and beauty often comes from adversity. The magnificent trees at Yosemite National Park are landmarks that have been around for years, challenged by cold winters, hot summers, fires, and storms. Yet their ability to survive has made them strong, with deep roots and impressive trunks. Only the strong survive in the forest, and those that survive can be appreciated for their beauty and presence. The beauty in marriage is also a product of what a couple has been able to overcome together. If you are fortunate enough to celebrate your fifty-year anniversary with your spouse, the closeness you feel will not be because of all the good times but more a product of the bad times and your ability to overcome together. I think the old saying "nothing worth having is ever easy" is very accurate.

I have recently had the privilege of counseling a young couple struggling with a severely handicapped son. They had all the hopes of a normal, healthy baby boy until some unforeseen events that left him—and them—with many huge challenges that would have lasting effects. When I first met with this couple many months ago, they were filled with hurt, sorrow, anger, and depression. Both were struggling with the events of the past eighteen months and trying hard to see God in the midst of their difficulties. This was not what they had planned when they started their life together. They had hopes of a very different life. But what they have found through this trial is the strength in one another and the presence of the Lord in a more real and powerful way than they have ever experienced before. I can't tell you why bad things happen to wonderful people. I can only tell you that we serve a good God, and He is good all the time, regardless of our circumstances. His desire for your relationship is one of tenacity, resilience, strength, and commitment. I assure you, marriage has the opportunity to provide you everything you desire in a relationship, but it will also provide plenty of struggles and challenges along the way.

Special Occasions

Misconception number six is that marriage is all about the anniversaries, holidays, and birthdays. Marriage is what is done between two people each and every day. Not long ago I had the opportunity to surprise my wife with a trip to the Island of Saint Kitts for her forti-eth birthday. I had planned it for a year, and she knew nothing about the trip or the wonderful couples joining us until we had left for our destination. My favorite part of the entire event, besides surprising her, was her birthday dinner on the beach by candlelight, looking back at the Island of Nevis. This was an incredible experience celebrating a wonderful lady, but it means nothing if I neglect her and our relationship the rest of the year. My role as a husband and hers as a wife is a daily, hourly, minute-by-minute commitment. We can be guilty of trying to make the weekends solve all of the problems built up from the weekdays. This will never work and will exhaust us trying. Just last week I was meeting with a couple in a very critical place in their marriage. They fight all the time and can't seem to make any progress within their relationship. As we discussed the past week, I noticed both of them were dressed fairly nice for a late afternoon therapy session. They explained to me that they were going on a date after the session and were excited for some alone time away from the pressures of home and children. I asked them if they ever argued during their dates, and they both answered no. They both made the effort to listen more intently to each other during these nights out—a skill lacking when they were at home. The marriage they want so badly, and need so critically, is only going to be a product of what they do day in and day out, not just during dinners out. Dating, dinners, anniversaries, and weekends away all are wonderful experiences, but without a commitment to each other in between these special times, your marriage will eventually suffer.

Not Your Grandparents' Marriage

The seventh misconception is that your grandparents had marriage figured out. This is not your grandparents' marriage. Marriage prior to the sixties was recognized as very traditional and a commitment seldom broken. Watch a rerun of family life in the sixties, and you might even see a couple sleeping in separate beds. Whether it was due to religion or social norms for that time, seldom did the people of earlier generations consider divorce an option, without very seriously considering the repercussions. However, what this also provided was many relationships that were lacking in depth or fulfillment. Couples stayed married because it was the thing to do, and this would often lead to a very unhappy couple just living a life, not for joy and fulfillment, but for convenience and obligation. I watched this with my own grandparents. Each visit I would watch them go at each other with bitterness and frustration. Seldom did they ever seem to get along. Their comfort and love for each other was obvious, but they didn't seem to enjoy each others' company that often. I don't know about you, but that is not what I want for my marriage, and I don't think this is what God had planned either. Genesis 2:18 says, "Then the Lord God said, It is not good for the man to be alone; I will make him a helper suitable for him." This tells me that it is good for couples to be together—good for support, for encouragement, for intimacy, for comfort, good for life. The good that is provided in marriage is not intended to replace what God provides, only to enhance it, and often be a source of it. God can and does work through your spouse.

When I think of what I want my marriage to be, I can't help but picture that old couple in the park holding hands and looking at each other with the love that has grown through the years. I would challenge anyone not to settle for your grandparents' marriage (unless your grandparents have a great marriage, that is).

Takes an Investment

And this leads me to my last misconception of marriage: that marriage does not take work or an investment. Many people today believe that a real marriage is one that involves two people in love, living a wonderful life together. Not unlike the movies we watch or the books we read, this concept is fiction. A marriage that stands the test of time requires constant investment. You wouldn't expect to have a productive career without investing many hours of time and energy to your chosen field; why would it be any different with your marriage? If you never invested in your 401k or savings account, expecting a big return in the future would seem a bit ridiculous, wouldn't it? Yet thousands of couples each and every day marry and believe that with enough money, a good career, and maybe children, they will live happily ever after. Unfortunately, this seldom is the case. Many years ago, Heather and I were visiting with her cousin about a marriage retreat we were hosting at our church. His wife seemed genuinely interested, but he, on the other hand, didn't see the value. They both passed on the invitation. Not long after that conversation, his wife decided to file for divorce. I remember visiting with him several weeks later and hearing him say, "I didn't see it coming, I had no idea." Just because things don't look bad doesn't mean they are good. In marriage and in life, you are either moving forward or backward, neutral just doesn't happen. If you are reading this book, you are making an investment in your marriage. Good for you. Don't stop. With great investments come great returns. God will bless your commitment.

My hope is that the act of marriage be seen in a more realistic light. This is not meant to discourage anyone about marriage. I believe marriage to be one of the richest, most rewarding relationships ever passed down by our Creator, a relationship second in value only to that of ours with Him. But in addition to fully appreciating marriage, we must also learn to understand the responsibility it requires for both spouses and to appreciate the work needed to build a healthy and happy relationship. When I became a parent, I was very unaware of the work that was to be involved in raising my two gifts from God. Still to this day I do not know if I fully appreciate the work yet to come. However, the work that Heather and I have done since the birth of both our daughter and son has allowed us to enjoy the wonderful young lady and man we see today. Our work has not been in vain, and we have reaped the rewards many times from our labor. As parents we continue to work, not as an obligation but as an investment in our children and their future. And we continue to work on our marriage, knowing that a rich and meaningful relationship continues to be produced now and in our future together.

Couple Application

1. With your spouse, list three misconceptions each that you had of marriage, prior to your wedding day.

2. List five interests that give you fulfillment outside of your marriage. Share them with your spouse.

Building Your Wall: Two Stronger Than One

Marriage is not for the weak. It takes a "never give up" mentality and a desire to achieve at any cost. Anything short of total commitment will open a door that will allow the enemy in. It is almost militant in nature. As a society, we have such a romantic almost Eden-like view of this union that words like "work" and "commitment" seem to be inappropriate or old fashioned. But the dedication and fortitude needed to succeed today in marriage requires effort and, at critical times, a plan. I believe the enemy and many in the world want to see your relationship fail. The world very often looks down on relationships requiring things like dependency, honesty, and openness. Yet to achieve the impossible and have victory in your marriage, at a time when many are not, you often have to start by building a wall.

Sometime in 2005, I felt led to pursue a degree and eventual license in marriage and family therapy. As God pressed this vision into my mind and heart, one of our pastors at First Baptist Edmond recommended I read the book *Visioneering* by Andy Stanley. Andy does a very good job of guiding people along the way to realizing and achieving their vision. He uses the story of Nehemiah to illustrate how God directs us through this process. As I read Andy's book, I couldn't help but see principles and lessons directly relating to married couples throughout Nehemiah's journey. One of my favorite chapters in the book of Nehemiah is chapter four. This part of the story has Nehemiah and the people pressing forward at rebuilding the wall damaged because of Israel's corruption and disobedience toward God. By rebuilding the wall, Nehemiah and the people were rebuilding their outward commitment to God and restoring the strength and confidence of a once strong nation. The scene starts out with ridicule and verbal attacks from Tobiah and his friends toward Nehemiah and the people at their effort at rebuilding the wall. You see, many did not want Nehemiah to finish his project (the wall), not unlike the many things standing in the way of you and your spouse having a healthy and happy marriage. Marriage is very much like warfare— it's you and your spouse against an onset of enemies determined to destroy your covenant to each other. But look how the people responded to their attackers in verse six: "So we built the wall, and the whole wall was joined together to half its height, *for the people had a mind to work*" (Nehemiah 4:6).

The mind is essential to accomplish a task or goal. Without a clear desire and attitude to succeed that comes from your thoughts, it will be almost impossible. As I prepared for my first triathlon several years ago, I recall 5:30 a.m. mornings where my muscles and body had no desire to run. Now this was not a full triathlon—more of a sprint—but to me it might as well have been the Boston Marathon. I was tired and could think of nothing better for me than to sleep another hour. But as I lay in bed with snooze button in hand, my mind would think of the race. I could see myself running and finishing strong. I could feel the sense of accomplishment that had not been attained yet, the anticipation of personal victory. This mindset got me up each morning in an effort to finish the race. I recently visited with a couple married just over five years struggling with a busy professional life and new baby, their minds filled with bitterness, anger, and resentment at what the other was or was not doing within their relationship. As we sat down to visit during our first session, it was obvious that each person thought the other was the enemy. Working together was not a concept they could grasp at the time. Neither of them recognized that they were at war for their marriage and that they could only succeed together but not without work.

Hard Work

The workers in Nehemiah had a mind to work. They would not, and could not, stop until the goal had been reached. This dedication and commitment would see them through when the world was working against them and it seemed impossible to move on. Your marriage is the same way; great marriages come to couples with a mind to work. This is about a person not being afraid to get their hands dirty to accomplish the task. As a young boy, I lived for about a year on a 40-acre farm. This may seem like a perfect setting for an eleven-year-old, but at the time I would have begged to differ. Between feeding animals, painting fences, clearing land, and burning all of our trash, it was no picnic. You can't live in these types of surroundings without a mind to work. Not that I didn't have great adventures, but the work could not be overlooked—it was just a part of the experience.

Many couples avoid the tough issues or work within their relationship, especially when it comes to the sensitive subjects like money and sex. We've learned somewhere to let "sleeping dogs lie." The problem is: eventually the dog wakes up. A real marriage tackles the issues no matter the cost. Remember, this is not an easy, carefree relationship (no matter what the world tells you) but one of work, effort, and labor to attain the goal. At the completion of counseling with one of my couples, we reviewed our time together and what made the difference in their time with me. Both couples reflected back on a specific time when I basically told them that I didn't think they were going to make it. Now this is not normally my practice, but when you see a couple repeating the same habits and self-destructing, sometimes you have to call a spade a spade. It turns out this is exactly what they needed. This was a call to action and from that point on, both spouses had a resolve and dedication to make their marriage work, at whatever the cost. You might say they finally had "a mind to work."

Together

Notice also in Nehemiah 4:6 (NAS) the word *we*. "So *we* built the wall, and the whole wall was joined together." The people built the wall together. Amazing things can happen when two people come together in a marriage to build the marriage and both have a mind to work. I would tell you that this has been one of the most beneficial aspects of my relationship with my wife. I am blessed with a wife that has a mind to work but also works together with me to overcome life's many challenges. When I get lazy and don't want to work, she pulls me back. As I mentioned earlier, at times it is extremely easy to avoid the real issues in marriage due to the busyness of life or just a lack of energy. It is a true blessing to have a spouse that will pull you back. Back in 2007, I was working on my master's in marriage and family therapy. This process involved many long hours of reading, writing, and class time. Couple this with a full-time career, extensive travel, a seven-year-old playing baseball, a ten-year-old in dance, a Sunday school class to teach, and a fifteen-year marriage to grow, and my life was somewhat busy. It doesn't help that up until 2006, I had experienced no formal background or education in the field of psychology. At times, this kind of journey can be exhilarating, but at other times, I felt attacked and beaten down. I remember coming home late one evening after completing one of my classes feeling extremely defeated. I could not see any way that I would make it through this college program. I felt as if I had no business even trying. I was a successful sales director with over fifteen years of experience in the energy market, a nice home, a beautiful family. Why would I want to enter a field I knew nothing about for a career with less financial upside than I had? The answer was quite simply: *because God called me to it.* Even with this answer, Satan has a way of using adversity to continue pushing us to ask the question. I can envision the Jews feeling the same way in Nehemiah 4:12. Verse twelve says, "They will come up against us from every place where you may turn." The scripture even says that they made this statement *ten* times. They were in panic mode and feared for their lives. Now I didn't fear for my life, but I can appreciate saying to yourself, *What am I thinking? I can't do this. I have no business being up on this wall. I could get hurt.* This is a perfect time for Satan to disrupt God's people and to turn us away from God's power and plan.

I met with a couple just today feeling very much the same as the Jews. He is a salesman that travels every week. When he is home he wants to unwind, relax, and have some time to himself. The pressure of his job and career can be overwhelming at times. His wife is in real estate and works when her husband's schedule allows. When not working, she is taking care of their infant child alone in many cases (at least this is how she feels). Seldom does she get any time for herself and usually expects little help with the baby from her husband. Their family lives out of town, and they have developed little friendship since moving to Oklahoma City. At every corner there is pressure. Both have needs, yet at times it appears they are competing with each other to have those needs met. Satan has done a great job in this marriage creating fear and feelings of being alone and defeated. Does this sound a little familiar? Yet at every corner of my battle and yours, we are not alone. We must first recognize that God has blessed us with our spouse. Second, we must learn to see God's presence in the midst of the storm. He has promised never to leave us, and we can trust in His Word. Two are so much stronger than one, but three is even better. Ecclesiastes 4:12 (NAS) says, "And if one can overpower him who is alone, two can resist him. A cord of three strands is not quickly torn apart." This journey is a "we" journey; you are never alone. A couple makes a stronger individual, and a couple combined with God makes a difference.

To Protect and Serve One Another

In order to take advantage of the "we" in a relationship, it requires action. Look at what Nehemiah does in verse thirteen: "Then I stationed men in the lowest parts of the space behind the wall, the exposed places, and I stationed the people in families with their swords, spears and bows." In verse fourteen he instructs them to "fight for their brothers, sons, daughters, wives, and house" and in verse sixteen, after the danger had passed, he continued to have half of the people carry on the work while half carried a sword. Lastly, look at the statement in verse 21: "So we carried on the work." Nehemiah stationed wives with husbands to protect and encourage them against attack, to allow them the peace to continue on with the wall. This is a great illustration of one of a key attribute of marriage—the ability and opportunity to fight for one another. Wives need to fight for the husbands and husbands for their wives. Don't let careers and busy lifestyles destroy your marriage. Back to my days in school, that night I came home ready to give up, my wife was there with sword in hand. She encouraged me with her words and told me that I could do this thing. It was as if she was fighting for me. That encouragement and support has been a source of great strength more times than I can remember. Her place in my life allows me to know she is always there to protect me and to support me as I build my wall. This is a job for both spouses and allows each to be stronger together than apart. When your spouse sees you fighting for them, there will be nothing they can't do or be.

But let us not soon forget that another is fighting for us as well. Isaiah 44:21 (NAS) says, "And Israel for you are My servant, I have formed you, you are My servant, O Israel, you will not be forgotten by Me." Regardless of the threats, exhaustions, frustrations, and stress, God was with His people as they built His wall. Nehemiah 20:4 says: "Our God will fight for us."

He knew, and the people knew God's promise. This fact alone gave each man and woman the courage and strength to go forward. There is a great deal of strength involved when we know God is for us, when we know He will pick up the slack when we can't go on. It is not uncommon for married couples at some point to feel helpless and out of control. We can feel defeated by our inability to change ourselves or our spouse. It isn't that the desire for a better marriage is lacking; it's the apparent ability to succeed that seems unattainable at times. But I have good news for you. God has the ability, and He is ready and willing to use it to change your marriage. In John 10:10: Jesus states, "The thief comes only to steal and kill and destroy; I came that they might have life, and have it abundantly." The life and marriage Christ offers for those who believe is one of abundance, because it is based on the resources provided by an all-powerful, all-knowing, all-loving God. This is why Christ came: so that you and I might have abundant life, now and for eternity. What a great promise!

In 1 Corinthians 12:26 (NAS) it says, "If one member suffers, all members suffer; if one member is honored, all members rejoice in it." Marriage should work the same way. When our spouses win, we win. Wives, have you ever been home when your husband received an unexpected raise or promotion? I would imagine his joy, confidence, and excitement spilled over to the rest of the family. But on the same token, we have all been guilty of taking a bad day out on the ones we love as well. It's okay, our spouses can take it, but it is prudent for us to not forget that we are in this together, flesh of my flesh, bone of my bone, till death do us part. If you take a tub of red Play-Doh and mix it with a tub of blue Play-Doh, you eventually get a mixture of the two. Have you ever tried separating the mixture so that you again have only red and only blue? Pretty tough— this is not unlike your marriage. You are one big ball of Play-Doh—not two—so try thinking in this way.

One Body

Lastly, we can't talk about working together as a couple without addressing the fear of being used by our spouse, of feeling like a doormat. Many couples fear loving the other at the cost of their own love and, truth be known, we all possess a sinful, selfish nature that comes out from time to time (or more). Chapter five of Nehemiah introduces us to a similar concept called usury. This is the idea of one person lending money to another at an excessive rate of interest. The people working on the wall did not have the time to tend to their own welfare and, as a result, had to borrow money from those with greater means than themselves. To do so they would have to mortgage their land, homes, and crops. If they failed to repay the debt, they and their families could become slaves. I can't imagine that this kind of pressure made for good workers. I would even say that the walls completion and its ability to be a symbol of God's strength and the strength of His people would not be possible without a resolution of this problem. Your ability to succeed in your marriage will not come because you have your needs met or got what you wanted. It will come because you gave your spouse what they needed. Think about it.

When human beings use others for their own gain, it destroys any opportunity for community and/or growth among others. We see this in business, sports, and even churches. To achieve great things in this life it takes more than one, it takes a team. But God knew this long before we did. Look at Romans 12:5: "So we, who are many, are one body in Christ, and individual members one of another." Paul is referring to the body of Christ, which all believers are a part of. By emphasizing one body, he is illustrating the unity we have as Christians with other believers. But as members one to another and with different functions (verse 4), we have diversity within the body unique and specific for the body.

But what happens when one member uses the other or relies too heavily on them? Look at 1 Corinthians 12:14-26 (NAS), making special note at verses 24-25: "But God has so composed the body, so that there will be no division in the body." When, as Christian brothers, we use each other for our own gain and purpose, there is division, and the body cannot function as it was intended. Now this isn't to say that marriage is always a 50/50 proposition. He does 50 percent of the work, and therefore, I do 50 percent of the work. Truth be told, marriage is very often more like 80/20 or 90/10. But at some point, the percentages have to change. A spouse always carrying 80 percent or 90 percent of the load will eventually give out and move to something else or mentally check out of the relationship. We see this process played out with Nehemiah. This well-oiled machine of people building a wall that many said couldn't be built began to break down because the workers were being used for the gain of their neighbors. It is this way in marriage as well. In Genesis 2, we see man's illustration of woman as "flesh of my flesh and bone of my bone" (verse 23). This brings up the idea of oneness or teamwork between husband and wife. A marriage is built to work together, to work with each other's strengths and weaknesses, stronger together than apart. Earlier in the chapter, in verse 18, God tells us "it is not good for man to be alone; I will make him a helper suitable." The first point to make special note of is what God calls as "not good." It is not good for man to be alone. God wants man to have companionship. This is His desire, and we are better, stronger people when we are with others (or we can be). Interestingly enough, this is despite our differences. Men and women are so very different, yet together God calls them "very good."

In the second part of this verse, the phrase "helper suitable" is used. This means a "power equal unto" or in other words "a match." God has made us a match in the form of our mate, not to be used but to compliment us. Instead of pushing each other down, we lift each other up. We are better together than apart, but only if we understand what "together" means. This is not about using each other for gain, but rather about working together to grow closer to God and to meet the many questions and challenges life brings. I see this principle played out time and time again with our daughter, Madi. So many times she needs the companionship of her mother—someone to talk with about her day, her feelings and emotions. Dad just doesn't cut it. But at other times, she is Daddy's girl, needing me to hold her or just tell her she is beautiful. As a team, we make a pretty good parent, and that is marriage.

This principle is probably one of the most missed in most young marriages today. I have seen many couples that can't help but see things from an individual perspective. They are so tied up competing with their spouse that they fail to see that "two have become one." If couples could start seeing their relationship more as a team sport and less as an individual event, changes might start happening. I see countless couples living separate lives but in the same house. He is focused on his career, yard work, poker night, golf with his buddies and men's Bible study, while she is occupied by her career, housework, ladies Bible study, Pilates, and girls' night out. The only time these two seem to get together is when there is a problem needing the attention of both spouses, and often we approach these problems with the same individual approach as everything else. But her insecurities are yours, and his fears are yours. When a couple can combat the attacks of life together, with exposed weaknesses and strengths, they can move mountains within their relationship!

One of the couples I counsel struggled because neither was able to reveal their fear to the other. She feared losing him, of being alone, of failing at yet another relationship with a man. He feared failing as a husband and a man, of never measuring up. Whenever the wife felt like she might be losing her husband, her first instinct was to try harder and be louder at times. This aggressiveness would cause him to feel like a failure, and he would then retreat to silence and solitude (duck and cover), which of course would escalate her fear and anger, and around and around they went. At one of our sessions, I had them both discuss their fears and how it affected their response and action toward the other. It was as if a light bulb went on, both started to see the other's fear and to recognize their own fear and its part in the relationship. This session was the beginning of this couple working together as opposed to alone. Picture a couple playing tug-of-war that eventually starts pulling from the same side and going the same direction.

Marriage is now and always will be about two people working together to make the best of their strengths and the least of their weaknesses. You need your spouse as much as they need you. You both make a complete package that is unique to all other relationships on planet earth. With effort and teamwork, you can both realize the wonderful gift that is your partner and together you can enjoy the many victories this life provides in and through the loving God that brought you together once upon a time.

Couple Application

1. List one activity each that you and your spouse could do together over the next two weeks.

2. Share one thing your spouse could do for you this week that would allow you to combat the attacks of life better.

Keys to Success

Marriage is not for the faint of heart. Many of us have been captured by the fairy tales of our youth and believe in living happily ever after marriages. At some point in your relationship, you fell in love. The emotions that accompany this experience are overwhelming and create some of the most enjoyable memories you will ever know. As a young man, I can recall the sweaty palms and dry mouth that accompanied that first date. I also remember New Year's Eve 1991 when I proposed to Heather. I could not stop shaking. I had plans to propose to her after dinner in front of a roaring fire, but I almost never made it. At dinner I was sure she could see my heart beating out of my shirt. The diamond ring in my coat pocket felt like it was going to jump out on the table by itself. I am not sure how, but I was able to overcome these feelings and wait for the setting I had originally planned later in the evening. The feelings of love are overwhelming, scary, and exciting all at the same time. It's almost like a roller coaster you want to keep riding. We all have experienced the excitement and emotions that come from love at some time or another.

I read not long ago about an Italian study where twelve men and women who had fallen in love during the previous six months were assessed. The research team found that the men had lower levels of testosterone than normal, and the women had lower levels of hormones than usual. It was as if the men were becoming more like women during dating, and women were becoming more like men. Another study reported by the University College of London found that neural circuits that are normally associated with critical social assessment of other people are suppressed when people fall in love. This may help us understand why we seldom notice the faults of our partners when we fall in love.

These facts and many others found through research and analysis of the human body help us understand why love has such an effect on people and also why marriages often struggle when the euphoria of a new relationship goes away. It is important to note that it is not a matter of *if* the feelings of love will fade but more a question of *when*. I have heard more than once a couple or individual proclaim that they have fallen out of love with each other or with their spouse. Often this is an example of love's effects on the body going away. It is almost like your body becomes immune to the drug of love. This isn't to say that you can't enjoy your marriage after the honeymoon is over, but it will take a little more effort. This is about the time you start noticing faults in your spouse or the effort of being a newlywed is quickly replaced by comfort and complacency. Men may say this is the time they noticed their wives moving from silk nighties to terrycloth robes, or women may say this is the time their husband started spending more time at the office. The best way to combat this metamorphosis is to know the skills that are needed to succeed. The same skills that worked in dating your spouse, and maybe the first year or two of marriage, are not necessarily the ones you will need in the future. Whether you are currently dating, engaged, newlyweds, or a seasoned couple, the skills needed to have a long lasting, happy, fulfilling relationship are the same.

A few years back as I closed in on my sixteenth anniversary with Heather, I was again struck by how much we can learn from the story of Nehemiah and his building of a wall in the Old Testament. The challenges he faced and obstacles he overcame to meet his goals can be directly correlated to what it takes to be successful in marriage today. In addition, the aspect of building a wall brings a very real illustration of what it takes to build a solid marriage. The challenge is to build a marriage that will withstand obstacles and attacks without breaking down. The goal is a marriage that will stand the test of time and, therefore, enable others to view what God has built and sustained.

My family and I lived in Connecticut for a few years, and I was amazed at the history. Some of the structures in that state have been around for over 300 years. If you have ever seen a 300-year wall, it is amazing to think how solid that foundation must be to stand that long. Think of all the snow, rain, and hail it has been through. Think of all the battles fought in its shadows. Think of all the visitors that have jumped, leaned, or ran on its structure. When they built things back in the 1700 and 1800s, they were made to last. Marriages for many generations before us were built the same way, a living testimony of success.

History

In Nehemiah 1:3, the author makes the following statement, "The remnant there in the province who survived the captivity are in great distress and reproach, and the wall of Jerusalem is broken down and its gates are burned with fire." This is a fair illustration of the state of marriage in our world today—great distress and reproach, broken down, burned. The state of the wall Nehemiah references was due to Israel's corruption and disobedience toward God (Nehemiah 1:7). How and why was the wall/city destroyed? As a quick background, around 587 BC, Babylonians invaded Judah and destroyed the city of Jerusalem along with Solomon's temple. This was the third of three campaigns into that region by the Babylonians. On all three occasions, Israel captives were taken and resettled in Babylon. Daniel, Shadrack, Meshach, and Abednego were taken in the first invasion (Stanley, 1999).

Cyrus, king of Persia, gave the Jews permission to rebuild the temple (2 Chronicles 36). Under Zerubbabal (Ezra 3) the temple was rebuilt, but the people refused to turn from their sins. During Nehemiah's days there were no sacrifices, Jews were adopting the religious practices of other nations. Political, social, and spiritual conditions were at their worst. So why was Judah destroyed? Second Chronicles 29:6 (NAS) states, "For our fathers have been unfaithful and have done evil in the sight of the LORD our God, and have forsaken Him and turned their faces away from the dwelling place of the LORD and have turned their backs." It could be argued that marriage is in the shape that it is today for the same reasons. We have sinned against God. We have been unfaithful and turned from God (Stanley, 1999).

The major problem today is we don't see the true value of marriage. It's not a priority. It's a resource, tradition, or option, but seldom do we see it as a true need. Look at Nehemiah 1:4: "When I heard these words, I sat down and wept and mourned for days; and I was fasting and praying before the God of heaven." Nehemiah was broken over the condition of his people. What would happen if we started seeing our marriages in the same way? Nehemiah took pride in his homeland and loved his people. To really care in this way for the institute of marriage, we need to take pride in it and love what it truly is. Find ten (even five) strong healthy marriages in your circle of peers. Not easy, is it? Wouldn't you like to be the one that made it, to be the couple that did it right the first time? To do it right is to succeed and to enjoy many rewards.

Don't get me wrong; love is tough. To love marriage is to love both the good and the bad, to love the past, present, and future. Doing it right is to love what marriage stands for and can provide. It stands for unity, commitment, dedication, and sacrifice. It provides strength, understanding, direction, comfort, and an opportunity to grow. One of the greatest attributes of God is His forgiving nature, and just like God offered His people forgiveness, He does the same for us in our marriages. Look at verses 8 and 9 in Nehemiah 1: "Remember the word which You commanded Your servant Moses, saying, 'If you are unfaithful, I will scatter you among the peoples; but if you return to Me and keep My commandments and do them, though those of you who have been scattered were in the most remote part of the heavens, I will gather them from there and will bring them to the place where I have chosen to cause My name to dwell.'"

First notice God's promise of consequences for unfaithfulness. Do we really believe that God will bless a marriage without the same faithfulness to Him? But the next verse is an even better revelation of who God is. In verse 9 it says that if we return and keep His commandments, He will gather and bring us back. For marriages to be restored, we must return to our commitment and keep our commitment to both God and our spouse. When God gathers and brings us back, this is a promise and commitment of His presence, protection, guidance, and blessings, just as He did for Israel in the Old Testament. This is the same principal as the vine and the branch in John 15:1-11 (NAS). In verse 5 it says, "Apart from Me you can do nothing," and in verse 7 we see that "If you abide in Me and My words abide in you, ask whatever you wish, and it will be done for you," and lastly, in verse 11 it says, "These things I have spoken to you so that My joy may be in you and that your joy may be made full." As a summary, for true fulfillment, joy, and contentment in your marriage, it starts with a commitment to Christ. Apart from this, you will miss the full measure of blessings God intended for you and your spouse.

When I proposed to Heather on December 31,

1991, I asked her to pray with me. Because of my past actions, this took her completely by surprise. You see, I had not lived the life of a Christian man in college, and I am embarrassed to say that many people didn't even know I was a Christian. But through watching the failed marriages of my father and the success of my mother's second marriage, it was easy to see the common denominator—Christ. I knew early on that to have a successful marriage, God would need to be the central focus. I prayed that night with Heather, committing my life and relationship to Him.

As we look closer at the Bible and the character of Nehemiah, namely chapter two, we see some of the characteristics needed for couples to make a marriage work after the honeymoon is over. Nehemiah used these same characteristics to build a wall. We are going to use them to build a strong marriage, one that will withstand the attacks of the enemy and allow victory in the relationship. We will discuss courage, prayer, humility, toughness (of skin), teamwork, and anticipation.

Courage

In Nehemiah 2:2 (NAS), we see the king notice the sadness of Nehemiah. He was the cupbearer for the king; for him to approach his master with anything but a positive disposition could mean instant death. But Nehemiah could not contain his grief. However, to approach the king with the problem was also to provide a solution. How would the king react to one of his employees requesting time off to rebuild a wall that the king's ancestors destroyed?

Fear could have left Nehemiah sitting and dreaming about what could have been. The only way he had a chance to accomplish what God had put on his heart was to take courage and to take the first step. What if he had not? I wonder how many marriages fail because no one took the first step. Maybe it's an argument that needs closure or issues of intimacy. Sometimes the hardest thing to do is to sit down with your spouse and talk. This isn't always easy and often takes courage, especially if it doesn't feel safe, but someone must take the first step. We see in verse 3 of chapter 2 that Nehemiah took the first step by approaching the king with his problem. I recall a recent joint session with a mother and adult daughter in conflict. Both women were very alike in looks and personality. They had drifted apart over the years due to numerous decisions made by the daughter from childhood that were not accepted favorably by the mother. Both women needed each other but didn't feel it safe to say so. In one of our sessions, I and another therapist were able to assist the mother in telling her daughter how much she loved and needed her. The daughter responded almost immediately by crossing the room and sitting on her mother's lap. As they both cried and expressed the longing they had for each other and their relationship, it was evident how much both needed this experience. It took a lot of courage for both of these women to express their feelings to each other. The risk of being rejected or attacked was very real. But the reward for taking a chance opened the door to a valuable and much-needed experience for both. This is also available for your marriage, but only if you have the courage to take the first step.

Prayer

Next, look at the king's response in verse 4 of chapter 2 in the book of Nehemiah. Once Nehemiah had the courage to confront the king, the king asked for his request. It didn't take God very long to reward Nehemiah's courage and faithfulness. But Nehemiah knew that without God's continued direction and influence, the impossible would not be possible. I am convinced that many victories and avoided disasters in my marriage have come as the result of prayer. Every day I pray for my marriage and my wife. Notice Nehemiah prayed before making a single request of the king. How often do you pray with or for your spouse? As we approach difficult challenges in our relationships, we must recognize the true source of power in our lives and pray for God's continued intervention and direction as we move forward. Nehemiah recognized this fact and was unwilling to make even a single step without God. This is a very critical aspect in realizing victory in our marriages today. I have found numerous studies that attribute both happiness in marriage and a decrease in consideration of divorce, with couples who pray at least weekly together. Praying for and with your spouse brings both power and protection into your relationship.

When I counsel couples, I like to start off the first

session with prayer. I pray that God would guide the process and protect the couple. I request the permission of each couple to pray, as it is not my intent to make anyone feel uncomfortable. In my experience most appreciate the experience and even request it in future sessions if I don't bring it up. I believe prayer impacts my counseling and draws couples closer. In 2008 when I formed my company, Counseling 1820, I referenced Matthew 18:20, which states, "For where two or three have gathered together in My name, there I am in their midst." I call on God's presence in my marriage, family, and career. What better resource for taking on the challenges of the world than the Creator?

Humility

When things go wrong, we very often look to God, but do we look with the same intensity as when things are going right? Nehemiah stepped out on faith and had the courage to move forward and as God blessed he responded. In verse 8 of chapter 2 in Nehemiah, he gives God the glory: "And the king granted them to me because the good hand of my God was on me." In this verse, Nehemiah is referring to all the resources granted him by the king for the task of rebuilding the wall. What was happening was not mere coincidence but God being God. In the movie *Facing the Giants*, there is a scene where the coach tells his team that they will praise God if they win and praise Him if they lose. I believe Nehemiah was going to glorify God regardless of the king's response. We need to approach marriage the same way. In today's fast-paced world, when life brings us adversity, it is usually our spouse that suffers most. It is very easy to take life's difficulties out on those to whom we are closest. I am sure we have all been guilty of having a bad day and then taking it out on our spouse or kids. But what would happen if we started praising God in the midst of our storms? God can only work when we give Him total control and all the glory. This is also the only way to be front and center when He works as well.

I never knew how true these words were until February 2011. I can honestly say that until that time, I don't believe I had ever really faced true adversity in my marriage. I had experienced some battles, but nothing would prepare me for what was to come. Around the last week of January of 2011, Heather became sick. She had a high fever, headache, and generally felt under the weather. Heather's symptoms were similar to the flu, so we assumed a few days of rest with a lot of liquids and antibiotics would do the trick. On Saturday of that same week, Heather was no better and actually seemed worse. That night, I took her to the emergency room concerned about her deteriorating condition. We would later be told by doctors that if I would have waited twelve more hours, she may not have lived.

Seeing my wife attached to so many machines, and in such a weak condition, made me feel helpless and lost. I struggled mightily to make sense of it all. *Things like this happen to other people, not me,* I would tell myself. Through the course of the next two weeks, Heather would remain sedated and on a ventilator, while very skilled doctors and nurses worked tirelessly to improve her condition. Never in my life had I felt so helpless. Each day was a battle. I clung to every scripture, every prayer, and every encouraging word from so many dear friends and loved ones.

All my life I have struggled with control. To have it is a comfort; without it is pure anxiety. I had no control over Heather's condition, and God was teaching me to let go and trust Him. I remember going to church the Sunday after Heather entered the ICU looking for worship and closeness with my God. I remember praying at the end of service and telling God that if He wanted to take her, He could. God did not need my permission. I knew Heather already belonged to God, but I also wanted to verbally commit to praise Him and follow Him, regardless of the outcome. This was a defining moment for me, a time when I gave up control and gained peace through my relationship with God, a time of total humility and trust. On February 13, 2011, after two weeks, Heather was taken off the ventilator and was awake. It was the first time I was able to see her beautiful brown eyes and smiling face. I cried tears of joy that day. God reminded me from this incredible journey that He is in control. God wants our love and devotion, and He wants us to humble ourselves and seek Him, in good times and in bad. When I needed Him the most, He was there, and He will be there for you and your marriage as well.

Toughness

Imagine Nehemiah's response when, after confronting the king, he heads to Jerusalem, ready to change the world. He was full of confidence after seeing God's work and totally committed to God's revealed plan and purpose. I would imagine he expected the people of Jerusalem to embrace his noble effort and to be excited about God's plans, as he was. But in verse 10 and then in verse 19, Nehemiah finds that not everyone welcomed him or his vision. Verse 10 says, "It was very displeasing to them that someone had come to seek the welfare of the sons of Israel," and verse 19 says that they mocked and despised them. These were people who liked things the way they were. Change was seen as a threat, and as we will see, they would do whatever they could to avoid it. This isn't unlike the feelings a frustrated wife might have when her husband doesn't see the problems in their marriage like she does. These are feelings like loneliness, hurt, and fear. It would be easy to give up, to respond to his coldness in kind, and to grow angry, resentful, and full of hate. But *don't give up*. Second Timothy 1:7 says, "For God has not given us a spirit of timidity, but of power and love and discipline." God has and will provide all we need to press on; our job is only to accept it.

In our marriages, things will not always go as planned, and as a couple, you will face adversity. Sometimes this adversity can be in the form of friends, careers, in-laws, or maybe even a spouse. But as Nehemiah illustrates, we must press on and ignore that which would keep us from our task. Nehemiah's task was to build a wall, and naysayers were not going to get in the way. Your task is to build a marriage, a task just as difficult and vital. Don't let others get in your way. Nehemiah could have taken what he heard and been frustrated, or even started to doubt the task before him. As couples, it is easy to doubt our spouse or ability to build a great marriage based on other's words or opinions. I am convinced the world does not want you to succeed, but press on—it will be worth it.

More than once in the past year, I have had the privilege of counseling pastors and their wives. On many occasions the pastor has caused difficulties in his marriage due to a secondary relationship. This is a time of hurt, pain, guilt, and anger for both spouses. The pastors themselves struggle with the loss of a job and the perceived ridicule of others, not to mention a hurt spouse and a damaged marriage. This is not an easy situation for anyone, especially young men committed to God's work. But pastors face the same temptation as bankers, politicians, and lawyers, maybe even more. It would be easy for these men to give up and face their failure as a man, husband, and Christian, but I don't believe this is what God desires. I believe He wants us to overcome, to face our insecurities, to face our sins, and, through His power, grace, and forgiveness, overcome and use this experience to bring others to Christ. I have been blessed to see this toughness from both the pastors I counsel and their strong spouses, and I know God will continue to use them going forward to increase His kingdom.

Teamwork

Rebuilding a wall cannot be an easy task. I am sure that the work of clearing the old debris is tough enough without building a new structure as well. Verse 17 and 18 sum up the motivation and teamwork needed before a task like this can even begin. "Then I said to them, 'You see the bad situation *we* are in, that Jerusalem is desolate and its gates burned by fire, Come, let *us* rebuild the wall of Jerusalem so that *we* will no longer be a reproach.' I told them how the hand of my God had been favorable to me and also about the king's words, which he had spoken to me. Then they said, 'Let *us* arise and build.' So they put their hands to the good work.'" Both passages use the words *us* or *we*. Nehemiah knew that he could not build this wall alone. It would take a team effort both in body and spirit. You cannot build a marriage alone either, however many have tried. Through the years, I have had the opportunity of meeting many godly women with husbands who have no desire to grow. This can be a very frustrating and demoralizing road for any woman. But you can't build a wall or marriage by yourself. So what do you do?

In the *Four Seasons of Marriage* (Chapman, 2005), Dr. Gary Chapman demonstrates several steps for influencing your spouse as opposed to manipulating them. Sometimes it's not about changing your spouse; it's about changing your approach. In Genesis 1:26-31 (NAS), God saw His creation as very good. A very good life (marriage) does not come without effort. But it is available, and it is God's desire for you. The key principle throughout Dr. Chapman's entire approach is *"positive choices lead to positive actions that result in positive feelings."* We have to choose to think differently about our marriage and spouse if we ever expect to see a change. Let me offer an example in my own life. In the last three years, I have worked hard to start a new practice. When your business is entirely based on people's ability to see you, the times and days worked are often dictated by your clients. I learned early on in the process that listening to other people's problems for hours each day was going to have an impact on my ability to listen to my own family's problems. At the end of the day, when I retire to the safety and rest of my home, very often waiting for me is more than one issue that needs my attention. It could be a financial decision, the discipline of a child, emotional support for Heather, or even upkeep issues with the house. Whatever the crisis or urgency, my ability to handle it with patience and understanding is often combated by my schedule and occupation.

I have a choice every night I leave the clinic. I know the temptations that await me at home. I have the opportunity to prepare myself to be there for my family regardless of my emotional and physical state. I also can prepare myself in other ways like a cup of coffee before I go home or prayer on my way, or both. By making the choice to be there for my family, my actions are affected. I can be a better father and husband, which is far more important than being a good therapist. In addition, the change in choices and actions then lead to a change in feelings. I see myself being more patient, I see my family more happy and appreciative, and I feel more positive about myself and life. It all starts with recognition and choice.

At times, however, the change has to come from someone else. I have been seeing a couple recently that has been married for over twenty years but have drifted apart. They have two teenage children but have been emotionally separated by a career that keeps the husband away most days of the week and some weekends. In addition, the wife is very concerned about the influence alcohol is playing on her husband. He drinks socially when away on business and will often have a few drinks when home. The wife feels that his ability to communicate with her and to show any true connection is deeply hurt by the alcohol. Any time she brings up her concerns, her husband feels attacked and shuts down. How can she confront something that might be damaging to her marriage when her partner won't listen? There is often a temptation in cases like this to become more aggressive or to hold something back, like sex, trying to force your spouse to listen and respond. This combative approach often fails. As a matter of fact, more times than not, it will make things worse by driving your spouse further away.

The thing to remember in a situation like this is that you cannot change your spouse, but you can be an influence. We are all individuals who have free will, but we are all also relational creatures that are influenced by everyone with whom we come in contact. Advertising companies know this as well as anyone. In marriage, manipulation doesn't work. We have to realize that we cannot make our spouse happy enough or miserable enough to respond the way we want them to. While you can't force your spouse to change, you can influence change in everything you do or say. Again, "positive choices lead to positive actions that result in positive feelings (Chapman, 2005)." This starts with choosing to think and act differently regardless of feelings and emotions. You can choose how you respond each and every day to your spouse and, in doing so, change your marriage.

Anticipation

The last characteristic for marriage we see in the second chapter of Nehemiah is anticipation. In verse 20 of chapter 2, Nehemiah makes the following claim, "the God of heaven will give us success." Nehemiah anticipated victory because he knew God. Sometimes it is easy to get lost and confused on the path of life. But knowing the God of yesterday and tomorrow allows us to trust in His perfect way. This is a great illustration of the good shepherd. In the twenty-third Psalm, God *leads me* in verse 2, *restores me and guides me* in verse 3, is *with me and comforts me* in verse 4, and *prepares a table for me and anoints my head* in verse 5. I can anticipate His presence wherever I go. Verse 6 says *goodness and loving kindness will follow me.* As a Christian, God is with you and has a perfect and specific plan for your life and your marriage. The covenant you have with God, as your Lord and Savior, is also the same you have in your marriage between you and your spouse. God designed marriage in Genesis. Therefore, He is uniquely qualified to guide and bless a couple that honors Him. We can anticipate this blessing and guidance just like Nehemiah anticipated God's presence with the task of building the wall. God wanted and planned for Nehemiah to succeed and He has the same plan and desire for you and your marriage.

Recently I asked a client what he wanted in a marriage. This client happened to be a very successful doctor. He immediately described a patient of his that had died this past year. He described an elderly gentleman he had known for some time. My client admitted to an envy of this man's relationship with his wife and how much it seemed to bring him happiness and contentment. He didn't know the financial status of this man, nor what he did for a living. He knew nothing about his faith, nor what he had accomplished in his life. All he knew was that this man was happy, and he loved his wife and she loved him. I believe God wants us all to be as happy as my client's patient, and I believe He provides a wonderful experience of this happiness for each of us, through our relationship with our spouse. We should anticipate this. We should seek after it. And we should not settle for anything less.

Couple Application

1. Out of the six attributes of marriage stated in this chapter, which is the strongest in your marriage, and which is the weakest? How can you celebrate the strong areas and make progress in the weak?

2. Take some time with your spouse over the next two weeks and discuss what your marriage will look like in ten years. Make it positive. Dream a little.

Communication: Learn To Speak French

Some time ago I was on a business trip in Alabama to visit a customer with one of my sales reps. One specific morning, we drove into a small rural town and proceeded into the office of a local trucking company. A beautiful young receptionist welcomed us and notified the owner that we had arrived for our appointment. During our wait the young lady asked Jon how he locked his car. At the time, it seemed like an unusual question, but I assumed she had never used or been introduced to a remote lock. As Jon politely showed the receptionist the remote, and demonstrated how to lock the car, the receptionist repeated her request. This time she said, "No, how do you lock your car? As Jon continued to persist with his demonstration of a car remote, it dawned on me that maybe we were having a breakdown in communication. Finally the receptionist repeated her request a third time, and we heard her ask, "How do you *like* your car?" Needless to say, this young lady's southern accent had thrown us both off a bit. Most of us know that communication is a vital part of any relationship. What we often miss is how and why communication works. Communicating just to communicate is not unlike me having a conversation with someone from France. We can have a conversation, but what will come out of that conversation is anyone's guess. And don't miss the fact that just because we don't understand someone doesn't mean we aren't communicating. This chapter is about communication done right. It is about learning to connect with your spouse in a way that offers the opportunity to increase trust, intimacy, and safety, all through better communication.

Lenses

One of the first things we must do to learn to effectively communicate is to understand the lenses of communication that exist between us and the people with whom we communicate. I only refer to them as lenses because, not unlike our eyes, we must pass through them and those of the other person. Let me explain. Let's say my wife and I are discussing the discipline options for one of our children. As I speak to Heather, it is important to recognize that I have some lenses, or influences, that are affecting my ability to communicate. First, as a man, I am more prone to take an aggressive approach to anything. Secondly, I grew up in a family that disciplined often, so I am comfortable with the concept. Third, depending on the child, I can be more prone to discipline my son but find myself less aggressive with my daughter. Right or wrong, all these facts, and many more, are affecting how I communicate to Heather on the subject of discipline. She can't see them, but they are still lenses that I pass through when speaking to her, and she passes through when speaking to me. Heather also has her own set of lenses as they relate to the subject of discipline. As a woman, she may tend to be more comfortable with a softer approach. She also may have grown up in a family where talking over problems was preferred over action. Lastly, she also may be prone to discipline our daughter differently than our son, or she may look at them very much the same way. Regardless of the specifics, there are also invisible lenses that make Heather who she is that I must be aware of when communicating with her. As a couple, the more we are aware of these lenses, the greater our ability to communicate in a constructive and mutually beneficial way.

I have a couple I am currently seeing in preparation for marriage. This will be the second marriage for both. The groom struggles with the memory of his parents failed marriage and the image of his father walking out on him and his family. Anytime he is faced with conflict within his current relationship, it pulls up very strong fears of failure in him, which can transform into anger. In addition, his ex-wife neglected him terribly, which affects his ability to trust completely in his fiancé and their relationship, in general. These are very real and strong feelings that are not always easily dealt with and can leave anyone feeling trapped and overwhelmed. Fair or not, these lenses exist in this young man, and the ability to communicate with him often requires a great deal of knowledge and understanding. It will be extremely important that his fiancé be able to see through some of the emotions that might be demonstrated and to also communicate in a way that offers support, encouragement, and trust in him and his ability. You can't change your spouse's past, but you can recognize the effect and compensate accordingly. This young man will probably always see circumstances differently than his bride. His bride's ability to understand and appreciate his view as being different than hers will help her communicate love, acceptance, and appreciation and will increase the level of closeness each person feels. She can't change him, but she can affect change in him.

Technology

Lately the use of technology to communicate has been a popular subject. I can't tell you how many times a couple has entered my office describing a fight they had between sessions. As they go through the traditional "he said, she said," I ask them the standard question of where and when did this fight occur. More times than not, I find that the entire argument happened through text or email. It has been stated by more than one source that over 80 percent of what we communicate comes from our facial expressions and tone. So, if we communicate by text, it could be argued that only 20 percent of the message is being heard. Not a great number if the subject is critical or a source of great tension within the relationship. I didn't grow up in the information age. Truth be told, I don't believe I had my own computer until my second child was born. But as I watch my children and other young people communicate through avenues like Facebook and Twitter, I wonder how well they communicate in person. I recall my own daughter just last year working on a new relationship with a specific young man. They would spend time texting each other daily. She seemed so comfortable in the relationship. Then one day we happened to see him and his dad at an event in town. I was taken aback by how awkward both of them appeared and generally how difficult it was for my daughter to speak to him. I realized that their relationship had been primarily through text and that neither of them had developed any kind of comfort level with communicating face to face.

In our relationships, we must learn to recognize the importance of expression and tone in communicating if we want the chance for something deeper. Electronic media, while very good for information and keeping up with the world, is not a good resource for intimacy. I would advise any couple to carefully scrutinize any and all subjects they discuss electronically. If important subjects come up, it is wise to request a separate time and venue for further discussion. When talking to your spouse, it is critical that you be heard both accurately and with sincerity. You have a much better chance of this in person.

Truth and Love

Ephesians 4:15 (NAS) says, "but speaking the truth in love…" this is a tremendous foundational principle in communicating within a relationship. Many times I see couples argue over truth or love but seldom fully grasp the concept of both in their relationship. As a wife, if you ask your husband how he likes your outfit, do you want honesty or love? It is very possible for the answer to be both. You want an honest opinion, but you want him careful with your feelings, protecting of your heart.

I see this dilemma played out in my own relationship when I ask Heather to read something I have written. She so much wants to lift me up and protect my fragile ego, but she knows I want her feedback and also want my work to be as good as it can be. Communication is most constructive and effective when we take both truth *and* love into consideration.

Honesty is a vital part of marriage. Without it, intimacy is almost surely gone, and along with it goes any opportunity for true closeness and security. A true relationship can handle the truth and even encourages it. Safety cannot be far behind when discussing honesty and the truth. If we want honesty from our spouse, we must also create an environment that welcomes honesty and makes it safe. I recall a couple married for over twenty years that came to me over past infidelity by the husband. As I spent time with this couple, I became aware of the wife's deep-seated need to be heard by her husband. She desired so strongly to express her emotions and feel accepted by her husband. It appeared she had been storing up so much over the years, and in session, it all came to the surface. Our sessions together were often filled with bouts of both tears and anger by the wife. Memories and emotions from many years past were brought to the surface. Her husband was not a bad man—quite the opposite. He was a strong Christian husband and father, served in a local church, and took great care of his family. However, over the years, he developed a habit of growing angry or avoiding any and all emotional expression by his wife. It wasn't that he didn't care for her. It was that he had no confidence in his ability to deal with these areas and instead would retreat or grow agitated. This would eventually cause his wife to avoid the issues with her husband, stuffing down all the emotions, and trying to ignore the pain. She never felt safety in the relationship. What neither of these two recognized was that the issues didn't go away; they just went below the surface to be dealt with on another day. They also missed the intimacy absent in their relationship, sacrificed because honesty and safety were unavailable.

Once we can create a safe environment within a marriage, we can then proceed with speaking the truth in love. Truth, while important, must be seasoned with love. It is so often about the presentation. If I offered you a beautiful steak for dinner on a garbage can lid, it hurts the overall presentation, not to mention your appetite. By learning to speak the truth, but in love, we grow intimacy in a way that offers renewed security and growth within the relationship. As a husband, my wife needs to know that I am always considering her heart first but also needs to know that I will offer the truth, and that she can trust me and ultimately our relationship. Don't miss the fact that we must learn to put love first, over truth. First Corinthians 13:13 (NAS) says it best, "But now abide faith, hope, love, these three; but the greatest of these is love." Truth with love offers a couple growth, intimacy, security and all the many things marriage was designed to provide. However, truth without love (or anything without love for that matter) offers bitterness, judgment, defensiveness, and all the many things that will ensure conflict throughout the relationship.

Buckets

During my business career, I recall a time when our management group was introduced to the concept of buckets and relationships within the company. The idea was that each of us has an invisible bucket that others either put into or take out of, which affects our overall self-esteem and emotional condition. For example, if people are constantly taking out of my bucket with negative words or damaging opinions, it can cause me to feel empty and with little motivation. However, if others are consistently putting into my bucket positive words and uplifting comments, it can cause me to feel more alive and capable. The general idea is that the overall balance of positive and negative words has a direct impact on the condition of your spouse and relationship. I think we can all agree that negative is sometimes much easier. I like to use the example of eating at a restaurant. I find it so much easier to complain to management about bad service than to proclaim good service. Negativity just comes easier, and we are naturally conditioned by our flesh to look at the bad over the good. Words, in general, have a tremendous impact on our ability to communicate, negative or positive. One wrong word at the wrong time can shut down a conversation immediately. So how do we talk about sensitive subjects with our spouse without experiencing a major shut down in the relationship? First thing we must do is to ensure that we have kept a healthy ratio of positive to negative words. Take an inventory of your words toward your spouse over the last seven days. Have you done a good job at balancing positives with negatives? It will be extremely hard to approach a negative subject with your spouse if they feel that a majority of your words are negative. Whereas, if they also receive positive or uplifting words, they will be more apt to listen and reflect on the subject you present.

Secondly, presentation is also critical in communicating sensitive or perceived negative subjects. When offering constructive criticism toward someone, starting your words with something positive and then ending with something positive can make the subject matter easier to handle. For example, if I was going to tell Heather that I didn't like the dinner she prepared last night, I might first let her know what an amazing cook I think she is (which I do) then mention my less than favorable opinion of last night's dinner then follow up with my appreciation of her being willing to make dinner each night. Notice first the imbalance of positive comments to negative. Second, notice how careful I structured my words (less than favorable versus didn't like) when offering criticism. This approach is not about dancing around the subject or sugar coating the truth, as some might believe, but is more about being sensitive to my wife's feelings and speaking the truth *in love*.

So many times in my counseling career, I have had the unfortunate experience of listening to two genuinely good people beat down each other with hateful and vindictive words. It was as if they were throwing actual weapons, like knives or spears, at each other with the intent of damaging. Somewhere, somehow, they have convinced themselves that they need to inflict pain on the other before they get hurt or as retaliation to being hurt in the first place. But these weapons of the tongue also bring pain and guilt to the one throwing them and can damage the relationship in a way that is not easily fixed. Jeremiah 9:8 (NAS) calls the tongue a "deadly arrow," and your marriage is often what dies from it. We must learn to guard our words and use them as tools to better our relationships, not as weapons to destroy.

Recently, a couple was discussing their week prior to our session. Earlier in the week, they had found themselves in an argument about the husband helping out around the house. This was a need the wife had expressed, and by not meeting it, the husband was communicating that he didn't care. As I further explored the exchange between these two people, I found that the wife was not asking for help but more demanding it. She would say something like, "You need to help with the dishes" or "Why don't you change the baby's diaper like I asked?" The response she often would get from her husband was a rolling of the eyes or mumbling under his breath. This communicated to the wife that the husband didn't care about the chores or about her. As we explored deeper the feelings of both the husband and the wife, we found that her requests seemed like demands to the husband. He felt talked down to and very much disrespected. He felt that the other things he had done had gone largely unnoticed and that no matter what he did, it would never be enough. The wife seemed a little surprised with her husband's reflection but was also able to recognize her role in frustrating him. We decided that by offering positive feedback and then asking for her husband's help instead of demanding it, she would find him more open and less hostile toward her.

Listening

Lastly, I would like to touch on the subject of listening. In my own experience, most of the breakdown in a couple's communication is directly related to the inability to listen. I will admit to being a very weak listener early in my marriage. As a type-A personality, I am always trying to multitask. It feels productive to be able to do more than one thing at a time. I pride myself on being able to achieve more in a short time than other people because of my ability to multitask. The problem is that people who multitask don't always make the best listeners. Whenever Heather would talk to me, I would find myself doing what I thought was listening while also preparing my response to her, wondering what was on TV, and thinking about dinner, all at the same time. Listening is about giving your undivided attention to the speaker. It's ensuring that the message being sent is the very one intended. It involves more than just hearing the words. Listening also takes into account tone, facial expressions, and context. When Heather talks to me, my overall focus should be to make sure I understand her. Notice the presence of sacrificial love in my statement. Listening is not about me or what I want but about Heather. It is hard to be selfish and a good listener. If we really care about the person talking, we will take the time to fully understand them by listening and to also communicate that we understand them.

My time as a counselor has allowed me the opportunity to improve my listening skills. As you can imagine, a poor listener makes a lousy counselor. I find myself working harder at understanding what my wife is trying to say. Often I find myself saying things like, "So what you are saying is…" or "What I heard you say is…" These phrases may seem like I am analyzing my wife; however, they have made a real difference in Heather's perception of me and my desire to hear her. Each phrase helps me clearly understand Heather with confidence but also allows Heather confidence that the message she is sending is the one she intends. What is even better is I feel more in touch with her and better understand her needs and frustrations, as opposed to trying to fix something. I have many of my couples practice this very exercise in session and ultimately at home. Each spouse is given three opportunities to share a feeling and why they feel a certain way. The other spouse then is instructed to repeat each feeling expressed by his partner, along with what they heard was the reason for the feeling. Sometimes the listening spouse will get it wrong, which then creates an opportunity for the speaking spouse to share another feeling and further clarify why they feel that certain way. This exercise is called listener/speaker, and it provides a very hands-on approach to the major functions of communication. When couples complete this exercise, they very often feel heard by their spouse and also better understood. Notice this exercise is not about solving anyone's problems but is totally focused on a couple's ability to speak and listen in a way that creates stronger connections and deeper communication.

A young couple I met with last year had been married less than a year and were in the process of buying a house. She was excited about the front of the house and the many landscaping options it provided her, while he was looking forward to the land and riding his horses in the open pasture. At a certain point in the buying process, the wife made a comment about *wanting* her husband's help with the landscape and keeping the house in good condition. However, that is not what he heard. What the husband heard was that she *expected* him to work on the yard each day and, therefore, would have to limit his horse riding time. But what the wife intended to say was that she would love to do some of the yard work together, as she liked time with him, but she also loved the fact that he had the opportunity to ride on the new land. This is an obvious "he said, she said" moment, where both spouses' inability to listen and effectively communicate allowed a moment of argument and frustration. Both spouses were focused on their own feelings and opinions over that of the other. Communication has a way of bringing out the best and worst in all of us. The key is to listen first and speak later. I am sure you have all heard the expression, "God gave us two ears and one mouth so that we would listen twice as much as we talk." Truer words have not been spoken when it comes to effective communication within a relationship.

One last point I want to make on the subject of

listening as it relates to conflict is to watch your words. What you say is not nearly as important as the way you say it. Communication already plays a major role in the success of your relationship, but when conflict occurs, it is magnified. When tension exists in a relationship, our ability to accurately interpret what our spouse is saying or thinking often becomes clouded. We start feeling attacked and can easily move to a more defensive position in the relationship. I often see this in couples that come in for counseling. There is so much tension and feelings of hurt that conversations quickly become defensive and competitive. A simple question like "How was your weekend?" can turn into World War III. At times of high stress or involving sensitive subject matter, it is important to slow down and make every effort to hear and to be heard by your spouse accurately. Very often what is heard is not what is said. Let me explain. I have many clients who like to hunt. They live for the time of year that allows them weeks on end, sitting in tree stands, waiting for that trophy buck to walk by their sites. It takes a special spouse to encourage and support this type of hobby, as it can require many days and weeks out of town. More than once I have experienced a conflicted couple with a wife complaining about her husband's passion for hunting. Sometimes this wife can show so much bitterness and anger it can seem like the issue is all about hunting. However, spend an hour with this couple and it becomes evident that the issue is not about hunting but about the husband's inability to spend quality time with his wife. Quality time *does not* mean Monday night football. As both spouses are better able to hear and communicate their true needs, conflict can be embraced and resolution realized.

Simply talk to each other. One of the biggest dangers couples face today is not how or when they talk but talking in general. In our fast-paced society, it is easy to get caught up in work, family, friends, and church, and forget to talk to each other. When a couple has no time to talk, it opens the door to avoiding or ignoring issues, holding back feelings, and mind reading, all of which leads to conflict. The less talking between a couple the more opportunities exist for problems. When problems are not dealt with, they are like weeds that grow roots deep into the soil. Once the problem becomes critical, the work needed to remove those weeds is often painful and time consuming and sometimes even impossible. I once counseled a couple married over thirteen years that would both admit to not truly knowing each other. She was a stay-at-home mom, involved in her local church, busy with the children and all their many activities. He was in the medical profession, worked fifty plus hour weeks, and would find himself away many weekends enjoying hobbies with friends and family, very often without his wife. This husband and wife had led separate lives most of their marriage. When they entered my office, the weeds had become so deep, neither was happy. So much damage had already been done. How do you make up for thirteen years of ignoring pain and avoiding issues? The answer is, in many cases, you don't.

In marriage, couples must take the time to talk. This was an easy task when you first met. I am sure you and your spouse spent hours just sitting together talking. In those days it didn't seem like work—it was effortless—and you probably enjoyed each moment learning more and more about your soon-to-be spouse. You don't have to stop learning. Have you ever wondered what you don't know about your spouse, even after all your time together? We can spend hours studying the stock market or hobbies like cooking or fishing but come up short with knowledge about our spouse. When something interests us, we often take the time and energy to learn more about it. Why not take the time and energy to learn more about your spouse? There is a pretty good chance the person you knew at twenty-five is different at thirty-five. We all change with age, hopefully for the better. Whether you know everything or not, the learning process will drive you closer as a couple, and you may find that you don't know as much as you thought. This is not unlike a Christian's search for a deeper knowledge and relationship with Christ. In his letter to the Colossians Paul calls them to "keep seeking the things above," and to set their minds on things above" (Colossians 3:1-2, NAS). A Christian should constantly be pursuing the things of Christ, or seeking after, never satisfied with the knowledge attained, always in pursuit of more because of the wonderful blessings that exist in Him. I wonder what marriages would be like if we were never satisfied with the knowledge we have of our spouse and were constantly seeking for more.

Above all, take the time each week to talk with your spouse. Set aside thirty minutes a day, twice a week, to talk about your day. Make this a time to share your feelings or discuss concerns you have. Make sure this is uninterrupted time with no distractions. Find a quiet space that is just for you and your spouse, and make it a habit. This investment of time in your marriage will pay dividends not only for you and your spouse but also for your entire family. Remember to talk, but don't forget to listen. Your marriage depends on it.

Couple Application

1. Set aside two times this week to sit and listen to your spouse. Make sure this is uninterrupted time with no distractions. Each spouse gets fifteen minutes of talk time while the other listens.

2. Make a point to tell your spouse one thing each day that you appreciate about them for the next week.

Expectations: For Better and For Worse

Marriage is not for the weak. With all the wonderful things that marriage relationship provides, it also can be a source of struggle. The beginning of this chapter may make you question the true benefits and hope that marriage can provide. Please know this is not my intent. I only want us to fully recognize what the marriage relationship is—good, bad, and indifferent.

Many times in my experiences with couples, I see the frustration and confusion surrounding a given spouse not living up to the other's expectations. I have a specific client who, after several years, was still hurting from his spouse's affair. In addition, he was struggling with his career and felt lost in anxiety and depression. He would state over and over "this is not the life I expected." I often wonder where and how we get these expectations that life should and will be free from conflict and adversity. I see countless engaged couples in pre-marriage counseling, and almost like clockwork, a couple will enter my office, and through a Q&A time, they will communicate their belief that sex will always be great, any problem they face they can overcome through their love for each other, and they will never question the love they have for the other. I personally would wish this on all my clients, but very often, reality is not quite that simple.

Somewhere, somehow we have convinced ourselves

that bad things happen to bad people, and since we are good upstanding Christians, in a so-called Christian nation, bad things should happen to someone else. After all, who wakes up looking for the sky to fall? We would rather just go through life expecting all to go well, basking in our ignorance to a point. I think people know, deep in their core, that life is rough, but I also think we can get caught up in the here and now and forget the work that is very much required to live. I counseled a young man recently whose wife had left him and decided she did not want to be married any longer. They had a young daughter together. This devastated the young man, and after almost a year, he was still struggling to make sense of it all. He would constantly ask me in session if I thought there was any chance she would change her mind. His ex-wife was already seeing someone else and had physically and emotionally moved on. But this young man continued to hold out hope that something would change. This position caused him continued heartache and pain. He would reach out to her again and again only to be hurt by her perceived indifference and coldness toward him.

I am very much in favor of marriage, and if two people want to be together, I believe they can. But in this case, only one person was committed to the relationship, and this meant the other must learn to move on. It was as if this young man was in the desert and could not take his eyes or mind off of the mirage. No matter the pain, discomfort or hurt, he had convinced himself that the mirage was real, but deep down, he knew it wasn't. You see, the fear of living alone and moving on were far greater than the hurt and rejection he was experiencing from his ex-wife. He had not yet realized that in order to move on in a positive way for both him and his daughter, he would need to embrace his fears. It was not an easy task but one that would eventually lead him to strength, peace, and new opportunities. But he first had to see the mirage for what it was—temporary.

The feelings we have for our spouse at any point and time are temporary as well. Whether they are feelings of great love and admiration or experiences of bitterness and anger, all feelings change. Think about the last time you and your spouse had a fight. Do you remember how you felt? I know when Heather and I have disagreements (notice I didn't say fights), I can experience feelings of annoyance, anger, bitterness, even rage. But I also recognize that these feelings are temporary, unlike the consequences of my actions at times. But do you also remember the last time you and your spouse felt a closeness or bond toward each other? As strong and wonderful as this feeling is or was, it is also temporary. I remember listening to James Dobson many years ago describe how stress and anxiety affects the human body—specifically, how the delta between our highest highs and our lowest lows can play havoc on our emotions and ability to manage stress. I remember riding roller coasters as a kid at amusement parks. Even today I can feel the anxiety, excitement, and nervousness of that first ascent to the highest peak of the ride. It was as if my body knew what was on the other side. Then to plummet straight down, maybe with a loop or two, would move my stomach to my head in about four seconds. This is a very real example of how our emotions can have an impact on our bodies. Mr. Dobson would go on to explain how our ability to manage our emotional highs and lows allow us to manage our stress levels and mental health. Fast forward to our marriages, when we are realistic within our relationships and we embrace both the positives and negatives, we allow ourselves to experience and manage life together, thus becoming stronger and gaining the ability to manage the ups and downs of life together.

Unfortunately someone, somewhere, came up with the idea that marriage should be something of fairy tales, with a Prince Charming and Cinderella in every house. Since we have been kids, we have heard stories that end in the familiar theme, "they lived happily ever after." The problem is that this most often is not the case. The Bible even makes this point clear for us in 1 Corinthians 7:28 (NAS): "But if you marry, you have not sinned, yet such will have trouble in this life, and I am trying to spare you." In this verse, the Apostle Paul is giving practical advice, not a moral or spiritual command. "Trouble" in these verses can be translated as "pressed together or under pressure." Sound familiar? I think most marriages I come in contact with have their share of pressure. It is hard enough to live single, much less with another. With two people come double the issues and problems that single life brings. Now this isn't to say marriage isn't good; just look at Genesis or Song of Solomon for that message. Two people bring double the blessings and strength as well. But my point is more about our expectations of marriage, especially early on in the relationship.

Trouble in marriage has not changed much over the years. The divorce rate still hovers around 50 percent, regardless of your religious affiliation or church attendance. The only new trend is we seem to be getting married later (average age is around twenty-four to twenty-six years). I tend to believe this is a product of people being more cautious about marriage, but we still state the same major reason for divorce as *incompatible*. What makes people think they were compatible to begin with? We are still expecting the fairy tale from our childhood, and when it doesn't happen, we close up shop and go looking for the next prince or princess.

But incompatibility is a fact. Men and women are different by design. These differences can be seen as compatible or incompatible depending on the looker. Let me explain. In most of the couples I see, opposites exist. She's a night owl; he's a morning glory. She's always cold; he's always hot. He never talks; she always talks. Sound familiar? Yet these can be seen as positive differences with the right perspective. As an example, my wife likes to sleep in each morning; this gives me a perfect opportunity to have my quiet time with God. It is all about perspective and love. Growing up, I always found magnets fascinating—especially the fact that two magnets facing each other with like poles could repel each other, like an invisible force field, but connect the opposite poles to each other and the force that holds them together can be extremely hard to break as well. I like this analogy when it comes to marriage: you give me two people with a lot in common and nothing to work for, and I will give you a potential marriage of limited strength and depth, with problems around the corner. But you take a couple with opposite interests and strengths (which describes a majority of couples), with the ability to see the differences as positives, and you will find a couple not easily parted.

So how do we learn to love the differences in our mates? It very often starts with the verb "love." But we first must understand what is meant by "love." Ephesians 5:25 (NAS) says, "Husbands love your wives, just as Christ also loved the church and gave Himself up for her." The love we are talking about is one of sacrifice, of selflessness, of servant-hood, not of scorekeeping or getting even. I am still amazed at how many couples have a figurative scoreboard above their bed. If he does this, I will do that. Because he didn't do this, I won't do that. Seldom does this course of action ever lead to a fulfilling relationship between two people. As a matter of fact, it is quite the opposite. Take love languages for example. I spend a lot of time teaching couples to love their spouse (or children at times) based on their love languages as per Gary Chapman's book. But one spouse will often refuse the others need for "physical touch" until they get some "acts of service" (as an example). The other won't give in on the "acts of service" without a little "physical touch," and never the two shall meet. It's quite a way to live your life together—and very frustrating. As long as you are constantly looking out for number one, the *full return* on your marriage will never be realized.

You see, marriage can be viewed as a commodity. Very often, the more you invest, the greater your return. When you think of how much time and energy we invest in money, jobs, children, friendships, hobbies, etc., it's hard to believe we don't invest more into our marriage, especially when you consider the return. According to recent studies, people with a strong marriage have higher incomes, live healthier and longer lives, have a natural defense against addictions, they are better parents, enjoy sex more, find life in general more fulfilling, and are more stable and secure people. Not a bad return, huh?

So the next question would be: how can I make a greater investment in my marriage? And this leads us right back to the word *love*. I could quote numerous scriptures that tell us about the importance of love. But the key is to know what love looks like and how to execute it. For this we need only to look at 1 Corinthians 13, the love chapter. You may find this verse very noticeable, as you can find it in just about every wedding in the continental United States. Sometimes, however, we miss the first three verses that tell us what love is "not." While verses 4 through 13 do a great job telling us what true love is, we would be wise to not miss Paul's descriptions in verses 1 through 3 of the same chapter.

What Love is Not

1 Corinthians 13 (NAS) verse 1 says, "If I speak with the tongues of men and of angels but do not have love, I have

become a noisy gong or a clanging cymbal." In other words, our actions must match our words, and when they don't, the impact is very loud and frustrating. I was seeing an engaged couple recently, and I gave them a task to do between sessions, nothing complicated. It involved making a list of the needs they believe their spouse (or future spouse in this case) had within the relationship. When we returned for the next session, the future bride had a well thought out, typed page of needs she felt her future spouse possessed. However, her prince charming had managed to scribble out a few bullet points on a notepad prior to our session starting. This was not an act of love and very much hurt this young lady, mainly because it gave her the perception that she was not important and that their relationship didn't warrant the time. Now regardless of your skill at "waxing poetic" to your beautiful bride, at some point, your words do little good to assure her of your love. The only thing that will change perceptions is your ability to show her genuine love. Needless to say, the next homework assignment had a little more focus for this young man.

First Corinthians 13:2 goes further to say, "If I have the gift of prophesy, and know all mysteries and all knowledge; and if I have all faith so as to remove mountains, but do not have love, I am nothing." This is a very common mistake I see with many couples today. We somehow believe that going to marriage studies or reading marriage books will win us favor or love from our spouse. It's as if we believe by going to a college library, we should receive a diploma. Love or knowledge in this case still must be practiced. I counseled a couple several years ago with a husband who had studied *The Five Love Languages* by Chapman, mentioned earlier. This man was convinced that the issues in his marriage could be solved if only his wife would read the book, and truth be told, the husband was holding back love for his wife, almost like a ransom, until she started speaking his love language. If motives are self-serving, they are not love. Spouses know when love is the genuine article. Have you ever tried on a fake Rolex? Do you think you feel different, walk different, and talk different when the genuine article is on your wrist? Probably so. There is no substituting the real thing, whether we are talking about watches or love.

Finally, in verse 3 of 1 Corinthians 13, Paul sums up the final point as to what love is not. Paul says, "And if I give all my possessions to feed the poor, and if I surrender my body to be burned but do not have love, it profits me nothing." Actions, while important, still can be void of love. Remember our engaged couple a few paragraphs back with the young lady who typed and organized a very strong list of needs she believed her future spouse possessed. A great list indeed, but unfortunately, she had a hard time committing to these needs, while her focus was squarely on the misgivings of her future husband. Yes, true love is sacrificial, but the motive must be selfless not "what's in it for me." I see so many couples focused on their own needs without much real concern for the needs of their spouse. It's a good thing the love we receive from Christ is not based on what we have done (or not done) for him. You see to gain your life (or marriage); you must lose your life.

I will admit to not always being great at putting my wife and her needs ahead of mine. Sometimes I find myself saying "what's in it for me." Truth be told, I can be downright selfish at times. It is easy to see how sin can take over and get the best of me. Take today for instance. Heather and I had plans to drop the kids off at school and then go to the local YMCA to work out together. This would allow me some quality time with her and also provide someone to hold my keys while I run. This morning Heather wasn't feeling so well and decided to not work out. So this threw off my morning workout and started me down the road to a foul mood and an eventually bad day. How dare I have to run holding my own keys (I know, pretty sad). Now, I recognize this is a choice. God is still God and is in control. How I decide to handle changes in my world is up to me—just like my decision to love Heather, not because of what she does or even who she is but because God commands me to love her. I may be put out or upset at times because things didn't go my way, but this is between me and God. My actions and attitude toward Heather should be void of this position and committed to love (the verb). In other words, *my feelings have nothing to do with loving my wife.*

So in summary, love is not about what we say, know, or do. Love is not something that can be faked or even something that we have to feel. Without a true commitment of sacrifice in love, demonstrated to us through God's son Jesus Christ, we will miss the wonderful blessings of marriage and the ability to touch our spouse in a deep and meaningful way. Expectations are one thing, but real commitment is quite another. So what does commitment look like with regard to love?

What Love is

First Corinthians 13:4-13 gives us a rather lengthy list of what love should and can look like within a relationship. It would be extremely easy to get caught up in what your spouse does or doesn't do well from this list. But I would like to keep our eyes on ourselves. Let's try to focus on the plank in our own eye as we "press on" to be a better spouse and eventually to impact our marriage in a productive way.

First, notice how Paul starts with "Love is patient." I don't believe Paul was ever married, but to start with patience is nothing short of divine inspiration. I don't think any spouse reading these words could argue that patience is not the easiest thing to accomplish in a marriage. Husbands, ever become impatient with your wife when you are waiting at the door to leave for church or dinner, and she is still working on her makeup, after an hour in the bathroom? Wives, ever struggle with patience when your husband leaves his dirty clothes on the floor or fails to put the dishes in the dishwasher—again? Patience is not easy. I think the issue of patience started when Adam and Eve sinned. From that point on, we stopped focusing on God and started focusing on ourselves. The key to patience is very often taking our eyes off of ourselves and putting them on God. It's the ability to wait, with contentment.

Do you really think that being on time to church or having all the dishes in the dishwasher is going to be a topic of conversation in heaven? Probably not, but I wouldn't be surprised if how we love our wives and respect our husbands is accounted for in some form or fashion. Patience in marriage is about priorities and the heart. We love (and are patient) because He (Christ) loves and is patient with us.

Next, Paul talks about kindness. I recently watched as a couple in my office talked about their difficulties getting along. While the wife was sobbing over the hurt she believed her husband had caused her, the husband sat about two feet from her as cold as an ice cube. No emotions, no regret. As a matter of fact, before she even finished her sentence, he was defending himself and accusing her of being over-emotional. This is not kindness and very often can be seen in couples that have been battling their relationship for long periods of time. As humans we can become callous when battles rage on. You might call it a form of PTSD where we walk around in shock reliving each battle, scared from the inside out and unable to make any sense of our emotions or life. Kindness is about being polite. It's about seeing a need and meeting it. You don't have to like someone to be kind. As a matter of fact, you don't have to even know them. We see people every day show kindness through their actions—donations to the poor, opening the door for a stranger, bringing meals to a couple with a new baby. Kindness comes from a heart willing to do what is right, regardless of feelings or emotions. In your marriage, you know what's right. Showing kindness is taking action.

"Not jealous" is the next thing on Paul's list of love characteristics, and this isn't necessarily all about other men or women outside of your marriage. I am currently counseling a young couple dealing with infidelity. One of the husband's major issues within his marriage is his wife's relationship with her parents. This particular husband is very private and prefers that issues in the family stay in the family. As men, we can be tempted to use this type of experience to exert our control. We can try to dictate when our spouse talks to her family or what information she gives out. Jealousy is the basis of control and is not love. We can miss the opportunity to work with our spouses to gain greater trust and connection despite this obstacle. Trust, communication, and acceptance are themes of love. Jealousy and control are not.

Paul goes on to say in verse 4 that love does not brag and is not arrogant. In other words, love is selfless and sacrificial. It is never about us but about them. If we speak more about ourselves than our spouse, this is not an act of love. If we inflate ourselves over our spouse, this is not an act of love. It's as if we believe that since our spouse won't call attention to our wonderful talents and accomplishments, we had better take care of it ourselves. But in doing so, we miss the very opportunity of being that source of strength and encouragement God designed husbands and wives to be for each other. One of the greatest joys of my marriage was the experience of watching my wife's strength when I went back to get my master's in marriage and family therapy. I think that just about every class I attended for the first time would lead me back home to proclaim to Heather that there was no chance I could do this. I was thirty-eight with a full-time job, traveling, teaching Sunday school, and trying to be a father and husband. It just did not compute. Yet at every turn, she was there to remind me where I had been and where God was taking me. She believed in me so many times when I didn't. She was my strength and encouragement. There is no way I got through school without her. I wonder where I would be if Heather was more focused on her own career or how little time I was spending at home or the money I was wasting going back to school. Her sacrificial love was the difference maker, and I like to think it made me a better husband as well. Ephesians 5 calls husbands to love their wives as Christ loved the church and for wives to be subject to their husbands as to the Lord. There is no room for bragging and arrogance in love and within a marriage.

Next, Paul tells us that true love does not act unbecomingly. This is a call for good manners and appropriate behavior within your relationship. Manners may seem like a little thing if you've been married for a few years, but are they? When we are dating, it seems appropriate to watch what we say or do. We are careful to give the other party the appearance that we are the "real deal." We very much want them to feel good about us and the relationship. Notice the emphasis is on the other person, not us. But once we get married, the makeup comes off and the cucumber mask goes on. As human beings we want to put our guard down and relax, to be ourselves, if you will. Now, I am not here to say this is all together bad. We need to feel comfortable around our spouse and have the ability to be genuine and relaxed, but to a point. When we cross the line of appropriateness and our thoughts go to ourselves and our comfort with no acknowledgement to how our spouse feels about our actions, we do not love. My stepdad has opened the car door for my mom since the moment they met over thirty years ago. I know this act does not define their relationship, but I also know it has and always will make my mom feel special, loved, and cared for. It isn't about comfort or convenience to my stepdad; it's about expressing love to his wife in a way that is appropriate and important to her. Now, I will be the first to admit that I don't open Heather's door every time we go out, but I know what is appropriate to her, and those things are in turn important to me, and this is love according to 1 Corinthians.

First Corinthians 13 goes on to say in verse 5, "it does not seek its own"—"it" meaning love. So love is about having a servant spirit and about being selfless. To me this specific love attribute mentioned in the middle of all these "dos" and "don'ts" by Paul is one of the central keys to a prosperous marriage. It you can't fully grasp, understand, and apply the concept of "selfless love," it will be hard for you to realize, appreciate, and enjoy the wonderful gift God created for us in marriage. "We love because He first loved us" (1 John 4:19). Christ is and always will be our marriage example, and His love for us is how we are to love our spouse. That He would die for the sins I committed yesterday, the ones I will commit today, and all my future sins is a testimony to how I am to love my wife. If sacrificial, my love can't be about Heather's actions or attitudes—good, bad, or indifferent. As a matter of fact, I show true love toward her when I feel she doesn't deserve my love and I love her anyway. Many years ago I was traveling on business (as I very often did), driving a long, lonely road somewhere in Missouri with one of my sales reps. Heather called me to see how my day was going and to give me a quick update on the kids. After our discussion, Denver asked me what Heather was doing that day. I told him she was mowing the yard, not really thinking it to be a big thing at the time. This caught him by complete surprise, and he could not believe that my lovely wife was mowing our one-plus-acre yard on this hot summer day, on purpose. I was a little surprised by his response, as this was not unusual for Heather. She very often mowed the yard when I traveled so that when I returned home, often not until the weekend, I could relax and enjoy my family. He then asked me how I managed to have a wife that mowed the yard. I now realized that this was not what most men experience in marriage and appreciated the blessings my wife provided me. I told him that someday I would write a book, and he could find the answer in chapter 7 (or something like that). Truth be told, verse 5 of chapter 13 of Corinthians is what I believe is the answer to this young man's question. Heather's act that hot summer day was one of love "not seeking its own." Now some might see the opportunity for me to take advantage of Heather's actions or for me to start expecting this type of action all the time. But Heather's action showed a trust of my love for her. She trusted me to see the love in her service and not to take advantage of it. Also know that Heather's desire to mow the yard was a response to the love I showed her as well. Women don't just up and mow the yard, even someone as wonderful as my wife. The selfless love I try to show Heather each day drives her to want to show me the same love. From a purely man perspective, it's almost competitive in nature. What a wonderful concept in marriage, each spouse trying to one-up the other in acts of love.

Couples have conflict; this is simply a reality. As a matter of fact, the most healthy, happy, and successful marriages have times of conflict. The difference is their ability to stay connected and to not let conflict define their relationship. Conflict is not the absence of love, and love is not the absence of conflict. But we can choose to love in a way that helps us more swiftly maneuver the obstacles of conflict within a relationship. Verse 5 of Corinthians chapter 13 ends with, love "is not provoked, does not take into account a wrong suffered." The NIV says "it (love) is not easily angered, it keeps no record of wrongs." Anger is an emotion, not right or wrong, but merely a response from a stimulus in our lives. Ephesians 4:26 (NAS) confirms this fact for us: "Be angry, and yet do not sin." I like to equate anger to a fire. When contained, it can do little harm, but let it get out, especially when the ground is dry and in need of moisture (not unlike some marriages), and look out. When I was in the fifth grade, my family lived on a 40-acre farm near Beggs, Oklahoma. One summer we had some church friends out to our land to play softball, fish, and fly kites. During this time of fellowship, someone's kite flew next to some power lines and got tangled up. When the power lines touched each other, they created a spark that fell and ignited our land. Within a matter of minutes a large grass fire had sparked. It took several people fifteen to twenty minutes to get the fire under control. We were lucky that day that there was little wind and we were able to contain the fire before it became too big. When sparks fly in your marriage, get control immediately. This may mean a "time out," a jog around the block, deep breaths, whatever it takes. Do not let anger destroy the field of your marriage. Love does whatever it takes to keep the fire of anger contained and small.

We also see in this verse that love has a short memory. In other words, love not only forgives, but it also forgets. This is not an easy task. We tend to hold on to the wrongs we have suffered for revenge or control. By letting go, we feel like we may be giving our spouse some kind of control over us or maybe condoning their actions. This is an example of Satan at his best. Often, by holding on to past wrongs, we pull them out for future arguments or disagreements, continuing to allow the fire of anger and strife in our marriage to simmer. I recall a specific couple who had experienced an act of infidelity in their marriage. The spouse who was cheated on already struggled with self-esteem issues, so the blow hit very deep. Over time, she was able to forgive her husband of his action, but she carried the grief, anger, and resentment for a lot longer. It would surface during any time of conflict or insecurity. The couple's ability to heal and grow was very much held captive by this wall she could not get past. Someone once said that forgiveness is a gift we give. It can't be taken, only received. When we love someone, we offer the gift of forgiveness and, with it, any record of the wrong. This is an act of grace and mercy not unlike what Christ showed us. It is an indication of true love.

Love "does not rejoice in unrighteousness, but rejoices with the truth" (1 Corinthians 13:6). True love within a marriage avoids sin joyfully and rejoices in the truth. A spouse committed to their marriage and to the love of their partner wants to do what's right. They are led by obedience and commitment, over feelings and emotions. They have a purpose and a commitment that supersedes any other calling in their world. Early in our relationship, even before our marriage, I cheated on Heather. This is not something I am proud of, but is a reality to where we are and where we have come from. The act occurred only once, and I held on to the memory of this event for several months trying to convince myself that revealing it to my wife would cause pain and hurt. The problem was that deep in the pit of my stomach, at the very core of who I was and wanted to be, I knew that a relationship without total honesty could never be what God intended. Heather didn't know what I had done, but I did, and so did God. So one Sunday after church, we went to lunch, and I confessed to Heather what I had done during our engagement and asked for her forgiveness. There has not been a tougher day in my marriage than that one. I cannot describe the hurt, pain, and anxiety I felt that day. I can tell you that it did not soon fade away. It took many months to repair the damage to our relationship, but it did get repaired. Hurt takes time to heal, as does trust. I was committed to gaining Heather's trust back and to repairing the damage I had caused her, at whatever the cost. I did what I knew was right, regardless of the pain or feelings to keep my secret hidden. I believe our marriage today is stronger and more fruitful because of this decision, and God continues to bless my obedience. Showing love does not always feel good, but neither did the cross.

Before Paul makes his final comments about love, starting in verse 8, he says "(love) bears all things, believes all things, hopes all things, endures all things." I see a little bit of resolve or a type of competitive nature in Paul's words in verse 7. You see, competition can be very good in a marriage—not necessarily between spouses, but a marriage that competes together is very effective. In churches Heather and I have attended through the years, there is often a time during the service where the pastor will recognize a couple that is celebrating a big anniversary. Usually this is a thirty-, forty-, or sometimes, even fifty-year mark for the couple being recognized. I have developed a habit of telling Heather at the time of the recognition that we can beat them and then trying to do the math (slowly) at how old I will be once we have matched this impressive mark. You see, I want to win in my marriage. I want to race to attain the prize, as Paul might say. What is the prize? In my book, it's a marriage that stands the test of time, a relationship that, after many years, still has trust, respect, passion, laughter, and all the other things that make life worth living. It's a marriage with many miles of road on it, both good and bad, experienced with another, that allows a closeness that few know or can understand (unless they have experienced it themselves). I want the dream marriage (versus wedding) that others look at and say, "I want that." And I want to hear God say, "Well done." To have this, I must not stop working. My marriage is not what it was twelve months ago, and my hope is that it continues to grow each day and each year and that Heather and I will continue to realize and enjoy the blessings of this relationship. Paul is saying in these verses that true love is doing whatever it takes. It's bearing all the burden with an optimistic attitude that is communicated daily to your spouse regardless of the pain, hurt, or difficulties. Love is basically doing what most believe is impossible, but nothing is impossible for God (Matthew 19:26, NAS).

Couple Application

1. From 1 Corinthians 13, what area do you excel in loving your spouse, and what area needs improvement? Ask your partner to confirm these strengths and weaknesses.

2. Take the time this week to write your spouse a love letter/note, or buy them a card expressing your love.

Differences: His Needs, Her Needs

As a product of divorce, I believe I recognized the concept of work in a relationship at a fairly young age. I had the fortunate opportunity to watch my parents' relationship end and also observe the success of my mother's second marriage, still alive and well today. You see, at the age of six, my father left my mother, younger brother, and me to pursue another life. Please don't get me wrong: not once did I ever question my father's love for me nor his commitment to have a relationship with both me and my brother. As a matter of fact, as I write these words, I am on a plane to San Francisco to play golf with both of them as we celebrate my brother's fortieth birthday together. The relationship we have today is a product of my dad's commitment and love through the last thirty-six years. But I also recognize that he made the decision to work as a father at that time but not as a husband. I also know from years of experience in the field of marriage that my mother had to have played a part in the relationship difficulties as well.

It is next to impossible to have a relationship problem without both parties contributing in some form or fashion. This, I believe, is an accurate view of all relationships: father/son, mother/daughter, employee/employer, etc. Let me explain. I have had many opportunities through the years to counsel adolescent boys and their families. Generally speaking, parents very often have a hard time seeing their contribution to the problem that caused them to seek counseling for their son in the first place. I recall a specific client who was struggling with pornography and rebellion toward his parents, specifically his mother. Through our time in session, I found that the client's time with his mother was very minimal and most often was shared with brothers and sisters. I encouraged the client's mother to plan some one-on-one time with her son in hopes of strengthening their relationship. It did not take long for all of us to see a change in this young man and his struggles, if only from some quality time from someone he dearly loved. You see, it is critical that we take the responsibility in all of our relationships to inventory our contribution.

Now, I am not saying relationship issues are always equal in contribution, only that both play a part or role. After the divorce, my mother would later marry my stepfather and model a marriage that allowed me to fully appreciate the concept of work in a relationship. I don't think I ever believed marriage was easy. As a matter of fact, most of my life, I observed how difficult marriage could be. Even with my mom and stepfather, there were challenges, especially with two wild, rebellious, and spoiled young boys, but the effort was always there on both sides. My mother and stepfather knew that marriage was not unlike a game. In order to win, you must use all your talents and understand the concept of teamwork.

Marriage is very much about teamwork, and each

member of the marriage has unique roles within the relationship. Many people today have a false concept of these roles. They believe a traditional marriage involves traditional or stereotypical gender roles. This includes the Neanderthal-like husband who watches sports twenty-four seven, belches at every meal, and demands a servant-like submission from his slave-like wife (ouch). The wife is often seen as a weak, powerless, domestic woman with cooking and cleaning as the highlight of her life. She is to have little to no authority in the home and cannot or does not make any decisions. With these concepts in mind, it is no wonder that many people today are looking for alternatives to the "traditional marriage." Regardless of popular opinion, this is not what God intended marriage to be. To understand the true meaning of marriage, I believe we must first start at the source, God and His Word, for each and every one of us. In 1 Peter 3, Peter outlines the role of both husband and wife.

The Example

> In the same way, you wives, be submissive to your own husbands so that even if any of them are disobedient to the word, they may be won without a word by the behavior of their wives.
>
> 1 Peter 3:1, NAS

A very important point to consider before we get too far ahead is to notice that verse one starts out with "In the same way." This is a reference back to chapter 2 where Peter proclaims Christ as our example. Before we can start looking at our roles as husband and wife, we first have to go to the ultimate example that will drive our expectations and standards as people and specifically, Christians. With Christ as the example, the pressure to be perfect can be taken off of us and our spouse. No matter how hard you try, you will fail. It's in our DNA. Our job is not to be perfect, as this is an impossible objective, but to strive to be Christ-like. This is a journey not a destination. Each step will please the Lord and make us better husbands or wives. Continuing on in chapter 2 verse 21, Peter says: "For you have been called for this purpose, since Christ also suffered for you, leaving you an example for you to follow in His footsteps."

Before Peter discusses how to live as a godly husband and wife, he first gives us the example, Jesus. Don't miss the fact that part of this example involves suffering. The marriage relationship is not an easy one. As a matter of fact, some have described it as the most impossible of relationships. Think about it: two people raised by totally different parents, in a different home, many times in a different culture, with different bodies, hormones, and emotions, not to mention different needs, wants, desires, and ambitions. It's a wonder any marriage ever succeeds. I don't think God ever intended it to be easy; otherwise, suffering would not be involved. But I do think God intended to bless marriages and those who honor its institution and follow the examples He set forth in His Word. Marriages that truly stand the test of time do so with the scars of battles fought and victories won. Their closeness and commitment didn't come from a ceremony, but from living a life of active commitment, each and every day. This brings to mind the service men and women fighting daily for our country. It's one thing to bond to someone during training or boot camp, but I am sure it is totally another to bond with someone in a fox hole with you, taking enemy fire, and protecting you as you protect them. This is a very real illustration of the commitment of marriage.

Not long ago, I participated in a marriage retreat weekend at a local church. On the last day of the retreat, I asked two couples married over ninety years combined to join us in defining what real success means within the act of marriage. Who better to communicate what it takes to succeed than those who have lived it? What I remember most about that entire weekend was the last thing one of the married women said to us that day. She stated very clearly and with an urgency in her sweet voice, "No matter what you go through don't give up, *it's worth it.*" You see, she had been through the battles and found victory on the other side. She knew what it took to have a real marriage, and she wanted everyone to know that it was worth the cost. I believe my marriage and relationship with my wife changed in February of 2011. My wife's illness and the concept of losing her changed me and how I look at her and our relationship today. This isn't to say our relationship wasn't special prior to 2011, but battles like these created in us a strength and bond that is hard to put into words. Think of an old tree with rings at its core for each year of life. These rings tell a story for each tree in every forest. I have been told that a ring can show a year of drought, forest fire, or disease. As each year passes, so grows the strength and girth of this old tree. The older the tree, the more obstacles have been faced and the stronger the trunk. Oh that this would be true of our marriages. No matter where your marriage is today, Christ is the answer to a relationship with your spouse that will stand the test of time and provide you and your spouse with the many blessings He intended.

Roles and Responsibilities

Now that Peter has set the standard for us in Christ, let's look at the roles and responsibilities that are described in chapter three for both husbands and wives. In verse one Peter calls for the wife to be submissive to her husband in the same way Christ is submissive to His Father. In my experience this is one of the hardest concepts for wives to grasp in today's culture. I have many female clients that cringe at just the sound of the word *submission*. Yet God calls each and every one of us (male or female) to submit to someone, whether it is the government or God himself. The key is often to focus more on the act and less on the person. When wives submit to their husbands, regardless of if they deserve it, they are showing their obedience and love toward our almighty God. In our world today, submission is often seen as a form of weakness or failure. We are allowing someone else to have control, power, or position over us. But notice the word *allow*. Submission is a voluntary action decided by the party submitting. Submission is not an attitude of slavery but of honor, respect, and selflessness, all traits found in the life of Christ. Christ submitted to death willingly, and I don't believe anyone with real knowledge of the circumstance could argue His strength.

The verse goes on to show how this submission can influence the actions and attitudes of a husband. Through submission husbands gain respect. This respect comes not only from a wife's action but also from her attitude and words. Wives, I cannot tell you how often Heather has touched my life with words like "Thank you for taking care of our family" or "You are such a great leader of our family." These are words of admiration and respect. Heather knows that they help me feel strong and successful as a man, husband, and father. She also knows the value of these words regardless of whether I am living up to them at the time or not. Men need to feel they are strong, that they are supported, and that they can succeed. God made us this way, and it makes us better husbands and fathers. Women often hold the key to this feeling. I had a couple once that was struggling with this very issue. At the end of one of our sessions, I asked to see the wife in private. I gave her a task for the week ahead. I asked her at some point during the next week to tell her husband that she respected him and everything he did for the family. I asked her to say nothing more or less and to leave the room after saying these words. I then asked her to report back to me at our next session on what his reaction was. I have done this exercise countless times before and the results are very often the same. In this specific case, the husband followed his wife from room to room asking more about what she respected and then eventually asked her to dinner later that night. The husband needed to feel respected so much that when he did, his reaction to spend more time and attention on his wife was immediate—and necessary.

Now I know men aren't always succeeding, and most often we fail more than we succeed. But if women continue to lift up men despite their errors, men will eventually overcome. Let me give you another example: let's say I am not very good at loading the dishwasher (hypothetically speaking of course), and let's pretend that loading the dishwasher correctly is a very important thing to my wife. When I put things in the dishwasher, my wife has a choice of honoring me with words like "Thank you so much for putting away the dishes" or correcting me by saying "Please let me put the dishes up; I have my own system." Now neither statement is wrong, but from a man's perspective, one has a greater ability to honor than the other. Again, one of the ultimate desires men have been designed with is that of respect, even more than love and affection. We (men) feel most complete and loved when we are respected. Don't be surprised if the husband you have always wanted appears from the respect you offer.

I recall a specific couple struggling in their marriage. The husband was out of work and already dealing with a lot of failure in his life. He had a very conflictual relationship with his father, he had failed with his first wife, and he was unemployed and struggling to not lose his second wife. Feelings of failure have a way of staying with you regardless of the circumstances, and once things go wrong, it can be a true battle emotionally to keep your head above water. In this specific situation, the wife had the habit of turning her fears into anger, which would lead to many bouts of verbal abuse toward her husband. This would then reaffirm his failure and would eventually lead him to a state of isolation and depression. I don't believe this was the intent of the wife, but she was responding to her own fear, and he was responding to his as well. If only she could have approached him from a different place, it could have changed their relationship. Both spouses in this example could have seen dramatic changes in their relationship if they would have just been able to understand and meet the needs present in the other. He needed respect.

In verses 3 and 4, Peter goes on to talk about the beauty of women inside and out. He says, "Let not your adornment be merely external but let it be of the heart." It comes as little surprise, I am sure, that men are visual creatures by nature. We are attracted to things that look good to our eyes. But beauty fades, and what is ultimately left is what is inside a woman. A long-term, healthy and strong relationship will always draw strength from the internal beauty of a woman. I am convinced that marriages would be changed all over the world if women spent less time in front of the mirror and more time on the couch talking and listening to their husbands. Men today so badly need this attention and admiration. This is not a character flaw but merely a design by God to make man the leader and head He intended for families across the world. I can hardly comprehend the impact that more confident fathers would have on young sons across our nation.

Peter goes on to say that a gentle and quiet spirit is precious in the sight of God. In today's culture, it is so easy to see the importance of appearance. For example, just glance at the magazines at your local supermarket. Most of the covers are filled with stories about plastic surgery, weight loss or gain, or what some celebrity wore that was fabulous or hideous. When so much time and money is spent on appearance, we can often put ourselves above God. This danger has been from the beginning, and God has not been subtle in His response. Look at Isaiah 3:16-24. The daughters of Zion were proud and walked with heads held high. In response, the Lord afflicted their scalps and made their foreheads bare. He took away things like anklets, earrings, bracelets, finger rings, mirrors, belts, perfumes, etc. These things don't seem to be bad in context of other evils in the world today. What we are talking about here is preoccupation with outward appearance as opposed to spiritual transformation and inward beauty. These women were making themselves to be their own God. Our God is a jealous God (Josh 24:19, NAS), and in this case, He did not stand for this type of idolatry. God, instead, wants women to influence their husbands in the Lord through their subtlety and submission.

Beauty is still important, and all you have to do is read Song of Solomon to appreciate God's view of a woman's beauty. But God also expects women to have an "imperishable quality" that Peter says is precious in His sight. The quality described in 1 Peter is one that is gentle and quiet. The word *imperishable* is translated as "incorruptible." You could say that a woman's true power and influence comes from within. Any man reading these words knows the power of a woman. I could venture a guess that each of us has a least one story of acts we performed growing up that were due to the encouragement of a special lady. I believe 1 Peter 3:1 (NAS) sums up this point better than any story. Look at the last part of the verse: "they (husbands) may be won without a word by the behavior of their wives." A woman's true beauty and power comes from within, and this is a beauty that will never fade. Don't get me wrong; men have played a huge role in telling women that they must look a certain way to gain attention and even love. But at some point, every man will come to realize that what they truly want and need from their life mate comes from the inside. Remember the two couples I mentioned earlier that had been married a combined ninety years? They knew this, and from my personal experience with both couples, they lived it and loved it each and every day. I want this for my marriage as well.

As I write these words, I cannot help but think back to the movie *My Big Fat Greek Wedding*. In one of the more popular scenes, Toula is talking with her mother over her frustrations with her father in regard to dating/marrying a non-Greek. The mother tells her daughter that, yes the man is the head of the home, but the woman is the *neck*, and she can move the head any way she wants. This is a wonderful reference to the power and grace God blessed women with.

The roles of husbands and wives are not about leader and follower, or boss and subordinate, but more about roles and responsibilities. In order to have a strong, growing, productive marriage, each member must do their part, within their God-given strengths and abilities, and with the guidance of God's Word, to enhance and contribute to the success of the relationship. It's not about you, or even about us, it's about Him.

Now let's look at husbands. Peter's direction to men starts in verse 7 where he calls men to live with their wives in an understanding way, as a weaker vessel. Peter's use of the word *weak* in this passage has nothing to do with physical strength or overall capability. He is referring to something of great value, fine, precious, or delicate in nature. If you own a crystal bowl, I would imagine you don't put it in the dishwasher when it is dirty. As a matter of fact, you probably wash it by hand with great care and attention. This is due to its delicate nature and true value. Like fine crystal, our wives were made by God delicate and fine, different than men. We are to strive to be understanding and to use caution in dealing with this precious, delicate, and very valuable gift.

Many times in our marriage, Heather has wanted to talk to me about a problem she is encountering. Now as a man, my first instinct is to try to solve her problem. As men this is our role and usually what we spend most of our days doing. But after many years of marriage, and many demonstrations of what not to do as a husband, I realized (and Heather has told me) that all she wants is for me to listen to her. This is not an easy task for me in that it appears to me that nothing is being accomplished. But what I am doing through listening is taking time and special care to give my wife what she needs—empathy and someone to listen. Through serving in this unique role effectively, husbands have the opportunity to grow closer to their wives in a way that I don't believe we experience enough as men. And don't miss that this is one of our many roles as husbands, no less important than protecting our family.

Many of the couples I see each day are challenged in this area. So many of the difficulties they face are about who's right and who's wrong, seldom about each other's needs. Just yesterday I was working with a couple of very bitter people determined to be heard over the other. Neither of them had any concept of what the other needed, nor did they really care at the time. They both gave me their versions of a somewhat small issue they had faced the week before that quickly escalated to the point we were discussing in session. As I recall the story, the wife had not been feeling well and, at some point, decided to go to bed with the eventual plan to miss work the next day. The husband confronted the wife while in bed and asked her if she was going to miss another day of work and if she thought this was a good use of her vacation/sick days. I don't believe the husband intended to come across as callous and uncaring, but to the wife, he did. She felt that she was inconveniencing him and that he cared little about her or her condition (not unlike washing a crystal bowl in the dishwasher). In my experience, the issue is never the *real* issue, but more the perception each person carries of the issue. To focus more on the other's perception, and less on whatever subject has you arguing in the first place, is to make real progress in the relationship. If your wife thinks you are inconsiderate, as far as your marriage is concerned, you are, and the only way to fix things is to understand her needs and *then meet them*. In this specific case and many others too numerous to count, her need is to feel valued, special, and fragile, and to be cared for by you in the manner dictated by this incredible value.

Finally in verse 7, Peter admonishes husbands to grant wives honor as fellow heirs. To succeed in life and love takes teamwork. There is no room for struggles of hierarchy and superiority in the marriage relationship. It is true that God has given husbands and wives unique skills and strengths, not to mention roles and responsibilities within their relationships. However, this uniqueness is designed to work together, not apart, and each partner is stronger and better because of the uniqueness of the other. Take flying as an example. The correct balance between thrust and drag allows an airplane to both move forward and up. If the balance is off in any one direction, it limits the airplane's ability to do what it does best—fly. This is very much the same in marriage. If you as the husband are not using the talents, intellect, and insight of your wife, then your marriage will be grounded or, at best, not fly straight. Take our family as an example. In Heather's world, dessert is not just for after dinner. Sometimes it can be for breakfast, and sometimes it can even replace dinner. Me being a type A+ personality, dinner must always precede dessert. Anything less would offset the balance of humanity. I need Heather to balance me and our family. Our kids benefit from two different viewpoints, and seldom do they mean the end of the world, even when it comes to dessert (plus sometimes it's just plain fun).

I am convinced that most men fail to fully appreciate the value that comes from a happy and content wife. When a wife is happy and fulfilled in her marriage, she is at peace to use her many skills and talents to affect your life in a very powerful way. And yes, I might even be talking about sex here, gentlemen. Do you really think your wife wants to give you the desires of your heart when she feels less than valued by you, her husband? I am sure you have heard the old expression "sex starts in the kitchen." In my experience, this is very often true. When a woman is happy and content within her marriage, she very often desires to return the favor to her man. Have you ever received a Christmas card from someone that you forgot to send one to? What is typically your reaction? Most likely, like me, you rush to send the forgotten friend a card before the holidays come to an end. People generally have an internal desire to return the positive actions of another. In your marriage if you want to truly be loved, then love. The problem is that many men don't know what it means to love their wives. We can often be guilty of approaching love like a home improvement challenge: if I throw enough money and time into it, I am sure it will get resolved. But loving your wife is not a problem to solve.

Gary Chapman said it best in his book *The Five Love Languages*, "We must be willing to learn our spouse's love languages if we are to be effective communicators of love." But I would also add from a more general point of view that wives need unconditional love. Ephesians 5:33 (NAS) says, "Nevertheless, each individual among you also is to love his own wife even as himself" and a few verses earlier in verse 28 it says, "So husbands ought also to love their own wives as their own bodies. He who loves his own wife loves himself." This is the love that so many women want and need. You see, this is not about selfishness or entitlement; this is about how God made women. When she is loved in this manner, she is all that a man could want and need. In other words, she will mow the yard. Men spend so much of their time providing financially for their family only to come up short because they are not providing what matters most: love. I dare any man to take a day off from work, or working out at the gym, or even spending time with the kids, to spend quality time with his wife. Study her, date her again, find out what really moves her, and value her as your prized possession. I promise this will make an impact.

Women develop this need for unconditional love at a very young age. I see this even today with my daughter, Madison. When things are busy and hectic in my world, I never feel close to her. She is busy with her thing and me with mine. Our worlds very seldom seem to connect. She's reading in one room, I'm reading in another. She's watching TV in one room, I'm watching in another. But many years ago when she was just a little girl, I started a tradition of taking her out to breakfast on Saturday mornings once a month. I will admit to not keeping up with this every month, but I do my best and seldom does too much time go by when we don't have our Saturday breakfast. This is our opportunity to connect, for me to devote my time and attention to her and her world. The results are nothing short of amazing. When Madison and I are able to have our time together and she can receive the unconditional love and attention she so often needs from me, our relationship is impacted. She will sit by me on the couch, she will want more physical contact, and she will want to share her world with me. I feel closer to her, and she feels closer to me. God made her to need this connection, just like He made your wife to need a connection with you.

In closing out this chapter, marriage is all about differences. There is no "one size fits all." Any successful marriage knows that understanding and appreciating the differences in one another is both a challenge and a blessing and very often one of the key components in a successful and lasting relationship. Let's face it—if you wanted someone just like you, you definitely wouldn't have married someone of the opposite sex. We were made different, male and female, husband and wife, for a reason. Enjoy the differences, embrace the differences, and be thankful for them. Loving your spouse because and in consideration of their differences is much different than loving them despite them. Love is a verb not a noun. Your love should not be conditional, but unconditional, and based on your spouse's needs (and differences), not always yours.

Couple Application

1. List one difference about your spouse and a positive aspect of this difference. Share with each other.

2. Discover each other's love language (www.5lovelanguages.com) and spend time speaking it.

Perception is Reality

Many years ago Heather and I were on our way home from church without the kids. As we left the church, a discussion started on our family getting a cat. I will admit to not being a cat person. Not that there is anything wrong with cat people, I just have not developed an appreciation for these animals. This is not a new discussion, as Heather grew up around cats and has always wanted one for our family. Throughout our marriage I don't believe I have ever said no to us having a cat. I have merely argued my case, effectively might I add, and given my opinion on this specific subject. On this particular day, Heather was more passionate than normal, and she was prepared to make a case for a family cat. As I recall the specific event at the intersection of Bryant and Second Street in Edmond, Oklahoma, what I witnessed could only be described as a temper tantrum of epic proportion by my sweet wife. Heather basically said, "I am a grown up, and I want a cat, so I should get a cat," kind of saying in essence, "you're not the boss of me." I have to admit the entire event made me laugh and Heather as well. I told her after that display, a cat was the least I could do. I only share this story to help set up the point of perception and reality. In a situation like this, it helps to understand that neither party is necessarily right or wrong, only with different perceptions. It is my job to not only see my view but also that of my wife's.

The battle of the sexes has been going on for many years. It is a competition that seldom yields any real winners or losers, especially in the area of marriage. Ask any man after an argument if he won or lost. Chances are if he won, he lost as well. I recall a young couple dealing with an alcohol addiction by the husband. One of the wife's biggest concerns was not knowing when and where her husband was and when he was tempted to drink alcohol. The problem, however, was that anytime the husband shared with the wife his temptation to drink, she would immediately stress about their future and his safety, barely able to contain her anxiety. You see her perception was that his sharing was an admission of guilt and eventual failure to keep sober. To her it was not an *if* he will drink, but more of a *when*. But what this young man truly needed was the ability to communicate his struggles and to have a wife that would walk alongside him in strength and resolve as he battled sobriety. The interesting thing is that I believe this is also what the wife wanted as well, but her fears often held her captive. Strength and resolve came for both spouses in this relationship when they were better able to understand the struggle and perception of the other. It wasn't about who was right and who was wrong. It was about understanding and empathy.

Understanding

Not long after my daughter was born, I returned from a long day at work to our tiny apartment in Tulsa, Oklahoma. Little did I know, this would not be a restful night in front of the TV. As I opened the door I found my two-month-old daughter and my twenty-six-year-old wife crying hysterically. I will be the first to admit that my first thought was to go back to my car and return to work. But it was obvious I was needed at home, so I stayed (yes, I was very wise for my age). It would have been very easy for me to get upset, as I had no idea how to help either of these ladies and I felt very much out of my league. I had spent hours and hours on prenatal classes, but I don't remember once getting advice on what to do in this situation. I later learned that my wife was suffering from a bout of pneumonia, and my daughter was struggling with a hernia. In eighteen plus years of marriage, I have continued to work on my ability to understand Heather and to not always try to solve a problem or fix something. In this specific situation, all Heather really needed was for me to take our child and to let her cry. Not overly complicated, but also not the first thought that went through my mind that night. The ability to understand your spouse's true needs and to then try and meet them is one of the most important things you can do within your relationship.

In general, God made men to work and to accomplish something. That is one reason why our occupation is so much a part of our identity. Ask a man who he is, and the answer you will most likely receive focuses more on his occupation than anything else. So it is not hard to see the dilemma men face when they meet up with a problem in their relationship that either they can't fix or shouldn't. I believe one of the hardest jobs we have as husbands is to listen to our wives. It's not that we don't care what they are saying, but to do nothing is counter to how we think as men. The same dilemma is found with women as well. Women were created by God to be a helper completer. But ask them to not be involved in every aspect of a man's world, work, or life, and the message received is hurt and distance. Yet men sometimes need to keep work at work. This is not always an indication of their wife's value, only of the man's need to keep focused and priorities in place. In marriage it is essential to work at better understanding these unique nuances of our partners.

When we first started dating our spouses, it was our mission to learn more about them. Dates were filled with questions, conversations, and dreams. We couldn't learn enough about our future spouse. This time of dating appears to be one part job interview and one part chemistry experiment. But at some point in our relationship, we stopped studying. True understanding comes not only from knowing our spouse but also from desiring to know them. It's not enough to know their favorite color we also must know when they are hurting and what they need from us. The more we know about our partner the more we are able to meet their needs and in turn have our needs met as well. When I see couples fighting and with high levels of anger and/or bitterness, I often find deeper issues just below the surface, very often to include: hurt, esteem, safety, etc. To fully understand your spouse is to understand that often the issue is not the real issue, and your response can be extremely critical to the growth of the relationship. Let me explain: let's say we have a couple named Bill and Lisa. Lisa, a thirty-year-old female, comes from an abusive family, and Bill is her second husband. She struggles with feelings of failure that have been present from a young age. She feels inadequate as a daughter, mother, employee, and wife. Bill, a thirty-five-year-old male, on the other hand, never received any kind of support or encouragement from his father. This is also his second marriage, and he is currently unemployed. He struggles with feelings of being worthless and inadequate as a man. When Lisa tells Bill that he is lazy and needs to clean up after himself, the hurt and pain of never measuring up is replaced with anger toward Lisa. He returns her words with comments about her lack of feelings and meanness toward him and the family. Lisa feels the reaffirmation of her failures as a wife and person, which quickly turns to anger as she yells at Bill for not having a job, which he then returns with comments about divorce, and quickly storms out of the house, reaffirming Lisa's fear of abandonment. As crazy as it might sound, this is not an unfamiliar scene to many in our world today. Do you see how each spouse reacts to the other with the baggage brought from their past? I would describe the above interaction as a dance. Each person takes a step that is countered by the other, and many times these steps lead to further and further emotional distance, not to mention distress. Regardless of the topic, the results are often the same: anger, bitterness, hurt, depression, anxiety, loneliness, and the list goes on. However, when one spouse or both truly seeks to understand the other and then responds to this new information with love, the moves change, as does the dance.

I am not saying that we will ever fully understand the opposite sex, but we should *seek to be understanding*. First Peter 3:7 (NAS) says, "You husbands likewise live with your wives in an understanding way." This directive is more about motivation and insight than true understanding. A better reference might be to appreciate your spouse's point of view even if you don't understand it. Appreciation can say, "I understand it is important to you," even if you don't understand why. In my own life, my wife needs me to talk with her on a consistent basis. When I don't talk with her, she feels like something is wrong, and this causes her to worry. I may never understand why silence equals concern, but in all reality, it doesn't matter. I appreciate my wife's need to communicate, and my job is to act on my understanding of this need. My action is my love toward her.

Understanding is a characteristic of love. First Corinthians 13:5 (NAS) says, "It (love) does not seek its own," meaning love has a focus on the other person and part of that focus is to understand. Understanding is defined in one source as "the ability to grasp meaning: the ability to perceive and explain the meaning or the nature of somebody or something." I find this particular definition interesting for two reasons: 1) the use of the word *ability* gives the indication that not everyone has this particular trait. Many may find the act of understanding to come naturally and without a lot of work, while others may find it extremely difficult and requiring a lot of effort if not training or therapy. 2) The definition also emphasizes the "meaning or nature of somebody." Take special note of missing words like *agreement* or *collaboration*. Understanding is not decision making. To understand is about the journey, not the destination. It's not about winners and losers; it's about intimacy and safety. As you seek to understand, you will find an awesome opportunity to exhibit love to your spouse and a very key attribute in realizing a successful and growing relationship with your spouse.

Empathy

Empathy is defined as "the understanding of another's feelings: the ability to identify with and understand somebody else's feelings or difficulties." We discussed understanding earlier, but empathy is another dimension of understanding. Notice the emphasis on feelings. As a husband, I can understand from a very general point of view that Heather needs to cry. Empathy comes when I seek to understand why or the feelings associated with this expression. Empathy has been a popular topic in the business community for several years now. You may have seen it referred to as "EQ." This is a reference to your emotional intelligence and can be recorded using various assessment tools on the subject. EQ has been defined (like empathy) as "the ability to understand others as well as one's own emotions and feelings." I have read in more than one publication that some of the top leaders in today's Fortune 500 companies have high EQs. I would argue that you could also find high EQs in successful marriages as well.

I had the opportunity to sit down with a couple

recently that had been arguing about an incident that happened on the drive to the clinic. The wife had been nervous because her husband was driving too close to the car in front of him. She explained her feelings to her husband and asked him to slow down to allow more distance between their car and the car ahead of them. The husband became agitated at his wife's request and proceeded to proudly point out his many years of driving and excellent driving record. He wanted no part of her telling him how to drive (as he had interpreted her request). Judging by the mood in my office, his explanation did little to calm her anxiety. I am not aware of any history of accidents in this particular woman's life that might cause her to feel unsafe or to even question her husband's ability, but sometimes the bigger question is how her husband could better understand the actual feelings she was experiencing. Through the husband's response, the wife described feelings of hurt, anxiety, lack of trust, and feelings of insignificance. On the other hand, the husband described his own feelings as including a lack of respect, hurt, and insignificance within the relationship. So who was right? With situations like this, neither spouse is right, especially when it comes to the relationship. For the wife to recognize and respond to the feelings and emotions of her husband would have meant being aware of her husband's need for respect and trusting him and his ability to drive safely, often despite her feelings of fear and anxiety. For the husband to recognize and respond to the feelings and emotions of his wife would have meant being aware of her fear and anxiety and slowing the car down to accommodate these fears. Both actions would have been a tremendous function of self-serving love and would have allowed each spouse to feel loved, noticed, and cared for. So often we cannot get past our own feelings of hurt, fear, anger, and frustration to effectively realize the other person's emotions or general point of view. We are stuck and very often unable to move forward in a positive way within our relationship.

The Bible has little problem explaining, encouraging, and even commanding empathy within all relationships. Look at John 13:24 (NAS): "A new commandment I give to you, that you love one another, even as I have loved you, that you also love one another." This is Jesus talking in these verses, and He is very aware (as He always was) of the events that were to occur in His future. The love He mentions in these verses is that of sacrifice. We are to love and seek to love, sacrificially. There is no room for "self" in love, according to this scripture. If we love our spouse, we will do all we can to sacrifice ourselves for them continually. This is a very complete summary of the concept of empathy. We are to strive to understand our spouse's emotions and feelings, not because we want to fix them and not because we want to win an argument or avoid conflict and not even because we understand them—but because we love them and because it is commanded of us as husbands and wives by our Creator. As I have stated more than once, love is something we do, not something we say.

Not long ago, my wife was struggling with hair loss as a result of her illness. The medical advice we received was that this was a normal process due to the medication and trauma on her body. We were given no real timeline for the process to be complete, and no one could tell us if Heather would eventually lose all her hair or just have severe thinning. I cannot pretend to imagine what this was like for Heather. Hair is so very important to a woman, and losing it, even for a short while, can be extremely dramatic. Heather was both brave and strong during this time, but I could tell it was taking a toll on her. One evening as we discussed her options and feelings, I went to the Internet to research possible options to help eliminate or at least slow down her hair loss. I presented these solutions to her in hopes that this would help her feel at least some sense of control in an otherwise uncontrollable process. My actions were not based on my own needs or wants but merely those of the one I love and care for deeply. I understood the feelings and emotions she was experiencing, and even though it was difficult to relate, I understood and acted accordingly. Heather told me later how wonderful this expression was to her and how loved she felt. This experience was not a product of our years married or my education or even our personalities; it was about loving my wife and taking the time and energy to understand her and love her through my actions.

Good empathy skills include the following: reading people, using emotions, understanding emotions, and managing emotions. As you improve your recognition and ability in these areas, you also improve your ability to act and relate to your spouse regardless of the circumstance.

Reading People

As I recall couples I have seen through the years, the general consensus is that our ability to read each other is much stronger when we first get married. We tend to spend a lot more time and attention on our spouse early in the relationship when we are trying to build something. Just like our relationship with God, we should never stop learning and growing with the one we love. However, at some point we get off track and decide that our knowledge and relationships are sufficient. As Christians we can be guilty of complacency. We get comfortable with our worship, Bible study, and fellowship. We can convince ourselves that we know all we need to know about God, His nature, and place in our lives. What a danger to miss God because we think we have it all figured out!

As far as marriage goes, I am not sure where we learned this trait, but taking for granted our spouses and our marriages can also be a critical mistake in the life of a relationship. Many a spouse has uttered the statement "I never saw it coming" when a relationship is at its end and beyond repair. Damage comes when we take our eyes off of the prize (our spouse), not necessarily when we experience the outcome.

I have a bad habit of always asking Heather if she is all right. I think I often read too much into a mood, facial expression, or lack of response. But this does not mean I should never pursue the cause behind her emotions. Yes, it is true that many times Heather needs her space. Her way of dealing with things is different than mine. Whereas I might confront issues head on when they occur, Heather is more apt to take some time to think through the issues before addressing them with me or someone else. Both positions offer many benefits, and neither is wrong. They are just different. However, differences are not a free pass to ignore the subject or cause of the emotions, regardless of the frustration this might create. I pursue answers because I want to better know and understand my wife.

I also recognize that my ability to read Heather accurately is not always present. Misreading can be damaging at times or can limit my ability to respond correctly to her needs. Not responding at all can actually be a very good response, but it depends on the problem and the person. My relationship with Heather is positively affected when I am seeking to know her and also when she is seeking to be known as well. The more Heather tells me, the more I know. My questions can be limited often just by her ability to communicate with me and her desire to share her thoughts, feelings, and emotions with me. Let me also state that I recognize that in a relationship, the ability to share one's feelings only comes from a safe, emotional bond. This takes time, trust, and the desire of both spouses to love and be loved by each other. But without this bond and the ability to both read each other and share, empathy is limited for both spouses, and so too is the relationship.

The ability to read your spouse comes with desire and attention. You will only know each other if you seek to know each other. This means making your spouse a priority. This is not unlike our relationship with God. God is constantly trying to communicate with each one of us. We can miss the signs and thus a deep and meaningful relationship with a living God if we fail to accurately read the Lord. How do we do this? We find God and the wonderful ability to read Him through a deep, detailed relationship with Him starting with His Word and prayer. In my journey to become a therapist, I went from the business world to a therapist couch in six years. As I look back at my journey I am able only now to see the wonderful path God designed and led me through. Unfortunately, it wasn't always easy to see the road during this journey. I had to constantly be plugged in, to be seeking His will and His direction daily, and to also be willing to wait on Him when necessary. God never disappointed, and when I needed Him, He was always there. Empathy in all relationships is the process, desire, and effort to be known and to know others. Start today.

Emotions

As a general rule, we are a very emotional people. We walk, talk, act, and respond based on how we feel each and every moment. Yet it is often these emotions and our inability to understand and manage them that causes destruction in our relationships.

Just this past summer, the family and I drove to Cape Cod for vacation. This is not a misprint—we drove. It took us approximately two days and 1,700 miles. As we arrived at our destination, I found myself confused by the many signs and turns leading us on to the Cape. Most of the trip up to this point, Heather had been assisting me with directions. We were using a combination of GPS, hard copy direction from the Internet, and memory from past trips. Despite all these resources, we missed our turn, and I proceeded to take out my frustration on Heather. I was short with her, blaming her for the entire mishap. Now this detour caused us to lose about five minutes of time toward our destination, but my reaction would have led you to believe we had lost an hour. Today as I look back at the event, I recognize the many things causing my reaction. On a long trip, your muscles ache, add the fact that traffic was heavy and we hadn't eaten, lastly the emotions of being close to our destination became overwhelming, and I snapped. That little voice in my head was saying, *What was she thinking? How dare she not be able to read a map? Do I have to do everything?* I had the choice to ignore my voices, but I didn't. I let my emotions manage me, instead of me managing them.

Emotions are not the enemy; as a matter of fact, they are a very real and positive part of who we are. I believe Christ felt and showed emotions during His time on Earth. After all, He was all man and all God. Look at John 11:35 (NAS): "Jesus wept." I have heard many people explain what Christ wept about that day, but what is important to me is to know that He did. To know that the same emotions I feel, enjoy, and, at times, struggle with today are known by Him as well, is a comfort and source of strength. A true intimacy within your relationship can come through understanding your emotions and sharing them with your spouse. I understand that this can feel dangerous and often feel unnecessary, but it can also be a doorway to intimacy you have never known. A quick note to men, very often women need to know how you feel. They need to know *that you feel* and to see it played out. In session I find so much power within a relationship when a husband finally drops his guard and shares his emotions with his wife. The closeness that this act provides cannot be expressed in words. A husband shows his strength, weakness, and trust in his wife when he shares his emotions. A wife shows her acceptance, admiration, and openness when she accepts him and all his feelings safely.

For women, emotions generally come more naturally than for men. This can be both a curse and blessing. On one hand it can be a source of great burden when you feel emotional and cannot explain or communicate why. There can be a tremendous feeling of being alone when your husband has no idea how you feel. It would not be abnormal to question your own feelings as a woman or think that something is wrong with you. Please know that in many cases, nothing is wrong with you. This is exactly how God made you, and it is good. Your emotions are very often the thing that seasons your marriage. Without them, marriage would be dull and boring. The key is to understand your emotions and to find ways to cope with the many highs and lows you may experience. Sometimes this will need to involve your husband, and sometimes it will not. You marriage will be strengthened when you can communicate your emotions effectively with your husband and direct him on how best to meet your needs. Trust me; he needs your help. As men, we were not blessed with the ability to know and understand female emotions. It takes practice and an education that sometimes only a spouse can offer.

On the other hand, as a woman, your emotions are a wonderful blessing to your family. Very often men find out who they are and what they are capable of through their wife's emotions. This is also where children can learn about the many advantages and opportunities emotions can play in a relationship. Remember, your marriage is your children's first opportunity to know the model of a husband and wife. Whether you are a man or woman, emotions are a part of who you are. It is not my intent to explain them, only to help you see that they are what you make of them. As couples, your ability to better use, understand, and manage your emotions gives you a more productive relationship and the opportunity to better understand who your spouse is and how to more effectively meet their needs. When your spouse's needs are met, you will find that your needs have a better chance of being met as well.

My ability to love as a husband should come directly from the example of love from my Savior. He loved so that I would know how to love. As I work on better understanding and relating to my spouse, I do it not out of obligation or expectation but out of obedience to my heavenly Father. My reward comes from what He does in me. What He does in my spouse is just a bonus. One of my first experiences with counseling came as a Sunday school teacher at our local church. I recall a specific young couple struggling in their relationship. He was working as a mechanic not confident in his ability as a husband or in the direction of his career or life at that time. She was struggling with expectations for herself, her husband, and their family. What did the future hold if they couldn't make sense of their marriage today? They were often involved in heated arguments, and at one point questioned their ability to stay together. I had the opportunity on many occasions to meet with the husband over coffee to discuss some of the many struggles he was facing. At many points during our time together, life seemed a little out of control for this young man. It seemed like everything he tried backfired. He felt he could never make his wife happy and questioned if she could ever make him happy either. During a visit to a counselor they were introduced to the book by Dr. Emerson Eggerichs titled *Love and Respect*. The concept of this book is to effectively meet the designed needs in your spouse God intended you to meet. In women it is unconditional love. In men it is unconditional respect. I very much love this book and recommend it often in counseling. Dr. Eggerichs's concept comes directly from God's word in Ephesians 5:33 (NAS). It says, "Nevertheless let each individual among you also love his own wife even as himself; and let the wife see to it that she respects her husband." What made a difference in this young couple's life was when they stopped looking at their own wants and needs and started looking at those of their spouse. This kind of change takes sacrifice and a desire to know and be known. This couple figured it out and went on to a wonderful marriage and continues to use what they learned to touch other couples for Christ. Your spouse's perception is your reality, so make it a priority.

Couple Application

1. As a couple, make a list of each other's needs within the relationship and compare your list. Do you know each other's needs? Are you working at meeting them?

2. Share with your spouse five things they didn't know about you.

Conflict: A Necessary Evil or Not?

I will admit that it is not easy for me to recall fights between Heather and I during our twenty years together. I am not sure if this is due to the fact that we don't often fight or if this is more a product of our ability to not take problems into the future. For whatever reason, I have few stories of Heather and me fighting. However, I will always remember one of our first fights prior to getting married. It was the fourth of July, and we were on our way to Riverside in Tulsa, Oklahoma to view the fireworks. We were engaged at the time and getting married December 19. As we drove together that warm summer evening, Heather looked over at me and asked me, "Are you nervous about getting married?" It didn't dawn on me that there was a right and wrong answer to this question. But me being a naïve, very young, twenty-four-year-old answered, "Yes, a little." This immediately put Heather on the defensive for the remainder of the night, worried that I was getting cold feet. It never occurred to me that this question was more than a question—it was a state of mind. I remember getting very defensive myself while Heather became emotional. This was a pattern we would grow comfortable with.

Conflicts, arguments, fights, disagreements—whatever you call them—they are part of marriage. No matter how long you have been married, there is a good chance you have just been in one, are in one today, or there is one right around the corner. People with successful relationships will tell you that it's not about *if* you fight; it's about *how* you fight, and how you fight *today* effects what you fight about *tomorrow*. Let me give you two examples.

First, let's look at couple A, married over thirteen years with two children. Their fights are characterized by sharp words, escalating emotions, and visits to the many infractions of yesterday (or the day/week/month before). Disagreements often move to arguments, which escalate to emotional fights for this couple. Seldom does a fight end in anything but physical separation and a cooling off period. The only thing that allows them to move on in life is to ignore the topic of the initial argument and to stay busy in hopes of avoiding the next disagreement. Now let's look at couple B. They have been married five years and have one child. Their conflicts are peppered with sarcasm and agitation, very often centered on the same unresolved issues from past conflicts. Like couple A, disagreements also move to arguments, but seldom do emotional fights ensue. Most arguments end due to one spouse's unwillingness to continue. The unwilling spouse eventually shuts down, causing the other to give up. As with couple A, seldom do topics of conflict ever get resolved. However, escalation is avoided in most cases, at least for today.

It isn't hard to see that these two couples could very likely be one in the same. When couples lack the ability to confront issues, they are doomed to repeat the same ritual again and again, with the only change being the temperature of the argument. More than once I have met with couples that had one spouse eager to solve a problem immediately, while the other needed to process things before moving forward with a plan for resolution. This is a perfect description of Heather and me. When I become aware of an issue, I attack it like a shark on a baby seal. The faster it can be devoured, the sooner I can move on to the next meal. No need to worry about trivial things like feelings, prayer, or wise counsel, just get in, get out, and move on. But fortunately for me, I married someone who needs to process and think things through before moving forward. Of course if I am not careful, my eagerness to find a solution can bulldoze right over my wife, providing an eventual solution but not necessarily the right one. Just any solution does not provide assurance that the problem won't come up again—and soon. It takes two to find the right solution. It also is important that you don't create bitterness and distance between you and your spouse while solving the conflict, which is exactly what happens when I don't take the time to let Heather process. Regardless of the conflict, couples have an incredible opportunity to work together to create peace in their marriage using their differences. It's important to remember that there is often more than one solution to a problem.

Conflict can create intimacy and closeness but only if you know how to fight. Here are a few key ingredients:

Confidence

Confidence plays a major role in the ability of two people to come together over a conflict. Whenever a spouse lacks confidence in themselves or their abilities, it can create dysfunction in the relationship. Let's face it—we all have areas of strengths and weaknesses. We can't be good at everything. It is inevitable that at some point you will enter an argument with your spouse and feel like the guy who brought a knife to a gunfight. Feeling inferior can cause a person to either disengage or over-engage, depending on the situation and specific personalities. There can also be temptation by the confident partner to take advantage of weaknesses in the other (see partner dominance below). When we lose the focus of a team in our marriage and start trying to win, we also lose the opportunity to grow as a couple and to find solutions using the strengths of two as opposed to one. Confidence allows both parties to feel they belong in the discussion. It allows each spouse to feel that their contribution is both necessary and encouraged. Confidence comes from inside of someone, but it can also be influenced by a person's partner as well.

Heather has a habit of wanting to take care of everything for our family. She is a third-grade teacher, and in addition to this very time consuming job, she feels obligated to buy the groceries each week, make dinner each night, clean the house, help the kids with homework, exercise, take care of her husband, have time with God, and generally walk on water. All these perceived obligations can get the best of her at times. Whether these obligations are legit or not, whenever she does not accomplish them, she feels down, like she has failed me, the kids, herself, and God. At these times her confidence is shot, and in this condition, it is hard for her to feel like part of a team within our marriage. She can mistakenly feel that she is the only one of us that struggles or feels at times like a failure. But this is very much not true. Her inability to feel good about herself limits our ability to be an effective couple and to have the closeness God designed. In Genesis 2 (NAS), God refers to the relationship between man and woman as "bone of my bone and flesh of my flesh." When Heather has confidence issues, so do I. It is my duty, responsibility, and joy to help her see her many gifts and talent. It also benefits me to help her see that she is more than what she does for me and our family. As her confidence is restored, so too is the strength and ability of our relationship, not to mention our ability to solve problems.

Assertiveness

Another key attribute in effectively handling conflict within a relationship is assertiveness. The idea of assertiveness being a good thing may seem a little odd to some. Assertiveness can be perceived by some as strong or abrasive, but this is not where I want us to go. Assertiveness is beneficial in a relationship when both parties feel comfortable and capable with confronting issues. It is about a safe relationship that allows confrontation as a vehicle for closeness and growth within the marriage. When both spouses feel that they have the freedom to bring an issue of conflict to the other and feel confident in themselves to address these issues, a relationship can grow and overcome whatever is put before it. One of the couples I worked with for several months had a problem resolving conflict. She had a habit of becoming aggressive when conflict would arise, while he would shut down. Each person didn't feel the relationship was safe enough to approach the other with honest and real emotions. She needed him to stay in the conversation, to make an effort to make her feel safe. He needed her to be more gentle and patient, to show him care, to allow for a safe environment for him to enter. Positive assertiveness was necessary for both spouses to have any chance for successful resolution, not to mention a full and complete relationship.

Avoidance

Any amount of avoidance within a relationship is not recommended. When couples avoid issues, they first miss an opportunity to further grow and develop their relationship, and second, the issue has a way of coming back again and again until it is resolved. Both spouses have a responsibility to create an environment that discourages avoidance. When one spouse avoids an issue, it is the responsibility of the other to help open up the subject and to recognize factors that might be causing the avoidance. Open communication and safety are key ingredients to minimizing avoidance. I recall a specific couple working on their second marriage. The wife had been abused in her first marriage and found avoidance easier than confronting issues. Conflict, to her, meant she was being attacked and felt unsafe. She would end arguments feeling a sense of guilt and responsibility. Early in the relationship, the husband needed to be very aware of her fears and to approach her with increased patience and self-control. Any anger or quick temper could be seen as unsafe, causing the wife to retreat and avoid any and all confrontation. As she perceived increased safety in the relationship, less caution would be needed as it was replaced by trust. Timing can be a helpful concept as well. Sometimes you or your spouse may not be comfortable discussing a subject at a specific time and place. I would encourage both of you to work at setting a time for coming back to the issue of question when this problem exists. This allows for processing of the issue but also does not allow for avoidance within the relationship. Sex, money, in-laws, children, and careers are all very popular issues that many couples avoid. They are also very often the issues that lead to divorce. Issues avoided don't go away; they just live to be discussed another day. Make a commitment to not let avoidance get in the way of your relationship.

Dominance

One of my first clients involved a young man struggling with self-esteem issues and a conflicted relationship with his wife. It is very common for both of these issues to exist in the same client. The client's wife was working on a secondary degree and was a very confident and motivated young woman. The client, however, was between jobs and struggling to find the career right for him and his talents. This is a very tough situation, especially for men, as we often draw our identity from our occupation. Very seldom can a couple with these types of differences handle conflict, primarily due to the perception of dominance one spouse has of the other. If your partner perceives you to be dominating, it has the potential of creating a gap in the level of hierarchy in the relationship, making conflict resolution difficult. When a couple comes together to communicate, regardless of the reason, both must come as equals, or at least, be perceived that way. When one is regarded as higher or lower than the other, it clouds the opportunity for a team approach within the relationship. The person perceived in the low position has a tendency to hold things back or to become overly defensive, while the person perceived in the high position has a tendency to be more assertive or demanding. Both must find a place where each spouse feels equal within the relationship and conversation. With the couple above, the wife needed to be aware of her spouse's perception of dominance and adjust her communication style and approach to encourage his participation and involvement. The husband can assist her by being cautious not to check out of the conversation and willingly share his feelings safely with his wife when he feels dominated.

All the keys listed above have the common theme of teamwork. Both spouses must come into a conflict with the other spouse in mind, while also being aware of their own contribution. Instead, very often conflicts take on a more competitive nature. I remember when I was a young boy playing football with my brother. It was so rewarding to have a younger brother. I never had to worry about being alone or finding something to do because John was always around. We could spend hours playing football, basketball, and baseball, seldom aware of the time or anything else happening in the world. I specifically remember our football games. We liked to play on the same team imagining an opponent on the other side. We were always on offense of course. I would play the quarterback, and John was the wide receiver. I think in those days I played the part of Roger Staubach, and my brother played the role of Drew Pearson. We would huddle up before each play and design a pattern to fool the invisible defense. It was great fun, and we always won of course. There was something about that team approach that always made us closer with much better results than other times when we would compete against each other. Let's just say Van Curen men don't like to lose and aren't very good at it either. This is the same approach that works so often with couples. You and your spouse are a team. Your conflict is not between you and your spouse but more you and your spouse against the conflict.

Let me give you a political example. Let's say that a very strong Democrat married a very strong Republican. Every four years the couple has strong disagreements about the government and candidates of interest that cause conflict within their relationship. However, the problem should not be bigger than the relationship. Problems come and go, but relationships affect our life and happiness for years to come. In this case the issue is not who to vote for but how the couple handles their differences. The couple is not competing against each other; they are competing against potential conflict and distance in their marriage. Together they can win despite the outcome of an election but only if they see that they are on the same team. Differences aside, what matters most is how you and your spouse treat and respond to each other in the midst of differences. If you trample your spouse because they are a Democrat, it will do little to improve the value of your relationship. It will also limit the peace you have within that relationship, regardless of politics.

1 Peter 5:8 (NAS) says, "Be of sober spirit, be on the alert. Your adversary, the devil prowls about like a roaring lion, seeking someone to devour." Satan is our ultimate opponent. The enemy would like nothing more than to destroy your marriage, and he will do anything within his power to have victory. I don't think it is a coincidence that Christian marriages today are being attacked like never before. The last thing Satan wants is strong Christian couples unified for God's glory and purpose. Being alert is the ability to be aware of attacks and the source of these attacks. When we attack our spouse during conflict, we can miss the fact that it is Satan at work. Our focus and energy needs to be combating him, not our spouse. A couple's ability to see themselves as a team with a common goal and common enemy creates a unified force. But let us also not forget that we are not alone. 1 John 4:4 (NAS) says, "You are from God, little children, and have overcome them; because greater is He who is in you than he who is in the world." We have power through our Lord within ourselves, and within our marriage. There is nothing the enemy can do that God in our marriage cannot

overcome. Victory in marriage comes from God.

Back in 1987 prior to graduating from high school, my father took me shopping to buy me a graduation gift. At that time the movie *Top Gun* had come out, and leather jackets were fairly popular. I remember telling my dad that for graduation I wanted a leather jacket. As we entered the store in Tulsa that day, I recall my dad walking up to a leather blazer and asking me if this is what I wanted. Now there is a very big difference between a leather blazer and a leather jacket. The generation gap that existed between me and my dad made it difficult to understand each other and to appreciate what I wanted in a gift. In marriage, perceptions are very often different between a man and a woman as well. She thinks football is boring; he thinks it is the best thing on the planet. She thinks *The Notebook* is the most romantic movie ever written; he thinks *Happy Gilmore* is better. She thinks a vacation should consist of room service; he thinks a tent and catching your own dinner is more ideal. Regardless of your likes or dislikes, both you and your spouse are bound to have differences. It is these differences that often result in conflict. However, when it comes to conflict, *perception is reality*. I don't care what the issue is or even your point of view. If it causes conflict in your spouse, it is a real issue.

My wife is currently out of town at science camp with my daughter. When she left I noticed several loads of dirty laundry in the laundry room and dirty dishes in the sink. Let's say that when she returned, the dishes were still in the sink and the laundry still dirty and on the laundry room floor. She would be fully justified to be upset with me for not taking care of these chores while she was away. On the other hand, I would be fully justified at not doing them because of my busy counseling schedule and never being asked to do these chores, which have been traditionally done by her. So who is right? The answer is both, regardless of which side of the fence you find yourself on in this situation. If Heather is upset about my insensitive nature and perceived attitude of servanthood toward her, then she is right, and it is my job to appreciate her position and try to improve the situation. My point of view, while important and necessary to understand, is not as important as making sure I understand Heather and that she feels understood and validated. From a conflict perspective, a couple can get caught up in who is right and who is wrong, when the answer is very often neither and both.

It is also important during conflict to examine the words and tone you use. If I want to approach Heather with a sensitive subject, I find a lot more success if I first compliment her or use a tone that is open, sensitive, and void of aggression than to just attack the issue head-on. I am not telling you to lie to your spouse, and I definitely don't want you faking it, but you would be amazed how much more effective you can be by taking a different approach to your words and tone. Let me give you an example. As a counselor, I have very odd hours, which allow me to be home at times when Heather is teaching. On occasion I use this opportunity to do the laundry. As a man, laundry is pretty easy. You have the jean pile, the white pile, and everything else. However, this is not quite how Heather approaches laundry, and at times I have put some of her more delicate items in the wrong pile. The other day Heather approached me gently to thank me for taking the time to do the laundry. But she also requested that in the future I hold off on many of her items because they require more attention. This could have been a very defensive and conflicting discussion between the two of us, but because of Heather's caring approach and sensitivity, I was better able to handle the message. I believe we all would like this approach when facing perceived criticism. I understand that words don't come easy for everyone, but your ability to communicate in a way that keeps the heart of your partner in mind, will help strengthen your relationship regardless of the conflict.

Conflict is never easy or fun, but it does not have to be fatal. As a couple, your ability to embrace problems together, being extremely aware of feelings, emotions, and the words exchanged, give you both a tremendous opportunity to grow past, and through, each experience. Successful marriages are those that stand the test of time. They are seasoned with the experiences of life, growing stronger with every passing challenge, and embracing each experience to grow. It is these experiences and God's presence in each one that strengthens the marital bond.

Couple Application

1. As a couple, rate each other on the four areas listed above. How can you improve in the areas causing conflict?

2. List two things you can do better as an individual during your next conflict with your spouse. Share these with your spouse.

A Few Words about Sex

Sex is not an easy subject to address. Whether at home, in therapy sessions, or even in church, sex is not a topic we are generally comfortable discussing. One of the reasons for this lack of comfort could be attributed to the conservative nature of our country. For me personally, growing up in the Bible belt, I did not experience a lot of frank discussions on the subject. I have to admit, most of what I learned came from friends, magazines, or television. I think parents of any generation often have a tough time talking about sex. Is it any wonder that many couples struggle with the subject? How can we effectively embrace sex in our marriage if we aren't even comfortable talking about it? In a recent Google search, two of the top ten reasons for divorce involved the act of sex.

Sex, or intimacy as I may refer to it at times, has been called a true example of God's existence. Who else but our Creator could create something so good and so perfect between a man and a woman? Before sin, God called the relationship between man and woman very good. But when sin entered the picture, so did the deterioration of this perfect union. Look how Adam and Eve's views changed after sin entered the picture. In Genesis 3:7 (NAS) it says, "Then the eyes of both of them were opened, and they knew that they were naked; and they sewed fig leaves together and made themselves loin coverings." Sex and the body were never intended to be something uncomfortable for God's creation. It was sin that corrupted such a beautiful act. Today this corruption continues to impact our ability to see and respond to sex within marriage. Couples attach sex to images on television or scenes from a movie. We can be guilty of seeing it as dirty or risky. God intended it to be a pure and wonderful way to express ourselves to each other. Sex outside of marriage will never measure up to what God designed when He created man and woman. When we have sex outside of marriage, it negates the very thing that makes a marriage relationship so spectacular: exclusive intimacy between a husband and wife. When we choose not to wait, we choose to have a second-rate marriage. I know, because I didn't wait. This isn't to say that I see my marriage as second rate. But I know that what God intended for my marriage was never fully realized because of the decisions of my youth.

In general, men and women tend to look at sex in very different ways. It is these differences that cause a large amount of conflict in the bedroom. Men tend to be very outwardly focused, relying on visual cues and touch, much more than women. Women tend to be more inward focused, relying more on emotions and connections. Combined, this can be a very powerful recipe. Approached separately, conflict is never far away. As men and women are better able to understand these differences, they create an opportunity to meet the desires of their spouse, which can then translate to their own needs being met.

One of the ways Heather and I do this in our own

marriage is to get out of town. At least once a year we go away for the weekend. It is our time to focus on each other and on our marriage. Sometimes it is just a trip to Tulsa for the weekend. The key is to get away from distractions. This time enables me to focus more on Heather and her needs. Heather enjoys time watching movies and loves it when we just lay around in a hotel room watching together. I remember one trip where we watched at least eight movies in a two-day period. Now this would not be my first choice of weekend activities, but this specific time together allowed Heather to feel more connected to me. But let me also say we did more than watch movies. This time also created a wonderful intimate connection between us both. My physical needs were met because Heather's emotional needs were met as well. For couples with children and busy lifestyles, I would always recommend weekends away.

Sex always should be seen as a gift. Something that can be accepted and given, it cannot be taken, held captive, or manipulated. To enjoy a true gift, is to enjoy the act at which it has been given. So many times I see couples playing games in their marriage when it comes to sex. I recall a specific husband that would request sex each night from his wife. When she would deny his request, he would pout, sometimes carrying on for days. This would then cause his wife to desire sex even less, his actions making her feel more as a servant, intended primarily for his pleasure and less as a partner. What this young husband needed was to feel wanted and desired in a strongly physical way, while what his young bride needed was to feel validated and prized in a more emotional way. Until we learn to help each other in specific areas of need, sex and marriage will be partners that struggle to get along.

I recall a specific anniversary Heather and I spent out of town. I had contacted the hotel many weeks prior to arrange roses to be scattered all around the room and bed. I was hoping that after dinner, it would be a wonderful surprise as we entered a normally ordinary hotel room. When we arrived at our room later that night, there were no roses to be found. I had to call the front desk to have them located and delivered, destroying my plans and the surprise. Now as wonderful as this gesture was, it was still not a guarantee of sex. It is up to Heather to offer, not me to coerce. When my actions create anticipation, without consideration of Heather's needs and desires, I move from a selfless focus to a selfish focus, and a positive intimate encounter is very often at risk. Truth be told, we did get a wonderful cheese and fruit tray from the hotel for their error and together scattered the roses all over the room. It was a great time celebrating a blessed marriage.

For Men

It has been said that to turn on a woman, you must start in the kitchen. I believe this saying has a lot of truth to it. Women become turned on not from what we as men do five minutes before intercourse but five hours or even five days before. Sex for women is a byproduct of our ability as men to meet their need for unconditional love. When we have a happy, content, fulfilled wife, we also have a wife more open to sex and intimacy. Most women experience intimacy through talking and spending quality time with their husbands. Very often by connecting with your wife in this way, you open up the opportunity of connecting sexually as well. When your wife feels that her needs are important to you, your needs will likewise be important to her. I have found that one of the best things a man can do to improve his sex life is to effectively communicate to his wife that she is more important than the actual act of sex. When a woman feels like the act is more important than the relationship, bitterness and resentment soon follow. I know what you're thinking, *But, Donnie, what if it doesn't work? What if I spend all my time talking and listening to my wife and we never have sex?* Ephesians 5:25 (NAS) calls husbands to love their wives as Christ loved the church. Christ's love for us, as the church, is not based on how we react to it; it is unconditional. We are to love our wives the same way. Sex cannot be a condition of our love. We must love regardless and hope that our wives will love us back in the same way. I promise the bond you share with your wife by loving as Christ loved, will far exceed the joy and pleasure that sex provides, and who knows, you might get both.

For Women

Men need intimacy to connect. Very often their ability to hear you and respond to you will be directly related to sex. I am sure this comes as little surprise to many women reading these words. However, it is important that women understand that sex is a critical need of most men, not for the actual act, but more for the validation. Sex to men says, "I am good enough," "I am desired," "I am a man." Men connect manhood and masculinity to the amount of sex they have within a relationship. Right, wrong, or indifferent, a wife's ability to make her man feel strong and validated is connected to her willingness and desire to have sex. It's not an easy task when it's ten o'clock at night and you just spent that last six hours chasing a two and four-year-old around the house, while making sure the laundry was done, dinner on the table, bills paid, and nuclear war averted. You lay down for bed exhausted and wanting to get some rest before the next day comes, when you feel the nudge of the less-than-romantic man lying beside you. This is a clear indication that one thing is on his mind. How can he not understand or even appreciate how tired you are, not to mention you feel anything but attractive at this point? The important thing is to not let Satan get a hold of this situation. It would be easy to see your husband as an insensitive jerk but an alternative would be to recognize that this action is an outward desire to connect with you, an expression of connecting, a longing to know you and be known by you, and only you. Yes, it would be nice if he said these words, instead of saying something like, "You want to?" but it doesn't change the fact that this is his way of connecting to you emotionally. It is also an act that will allow him to more effectively open up to your needs. I know, it is not a perfect situation, but it is very possible that by meeting his need you will also create the opportunity to meet your own.

Communication

Talking about sex is never easy. Sure, we might talk with our friends or relatives of the same sex, but talking about it with the opposite sex is a different thing. I find that in marriage, sex is very seldom discussed. We have convinced ourselves that sex in a relationship just happens. We shouldn't have to work at it; it should come naturally. It is always a sign of trouble when I find couples in pre-marriage counseling convinced that sex will never be an issue in their relationship. This just is not the case. At some point in your relationship, sex will be a source of conflict. It is not a matter of if but when. However, we have a wonderful opportunity to prepare for this conflict by learning to talk about sex with our spouse. Couples should be free to discuss what they like, dislike, need, and want from sex. I understand this can be difficult. It is for me as well. I find it extremely difficult to talk to Heather about something so personal. What if I come across as selfish, or what if I embarrass her? It always seems so inappropriate. There never seems to be a good time to talk about sex. However, with discussion also comes greater opportunity for intimacy, both physical and emotional.

If you haven't already, talk with your spouse about how their family dealt with the subject growing up. Was it discussed or just ignored? How was sex introduced? Was it ever seen in a positive light? I have a friend who at one point was experiencing difficulty with sex in his marriage. He felt his wife never initiated sex and, at times, wondered if she even liked it. Through therapy, they were both able to recognize some of his wife's negative opinions of sex developed at a very early age. Sex in her family was always seen as something dirty or bad. To have sex, in any context, was seen as something inappropriate and improper. These feelings followed this young lady into her marriage. It made it difficult to freely give and take from her husband sexually without feelings of guilt and shame. This situation is not uncommon between a husband and wife and needs to be discussed. Talking can help lead to visible improvements. However, if problems persist it can also be beneficial to see someone specializing in this area. Also talk to your spouse about how you feel about your sex life as a couple. What are your favorite intimate memories together? What are your least favorites? It is important to know what your spouse likes and does not like. This is an easy way to reflect and to enjoy a trip down memory lane with your partner. Keep in mind that this is not a time for criticism. The purpose is to grow in comfort as a couple on the subject, while also learning more about pleasing each other. Very often this conversation can lead to fantasies and desires for future sexual encounters. Fantasy within marriage is not a bad thing. As a matter of fact it can be a great thing. Imagine the opportunity to make your wife or husband's dreams come true sexually. Also imagine the level of intimacy and emotional connection that can result from such an experience. Communication is very often the key.

Lastly, get good at talking to your spouse consistently about what you want and need. This is good advice for all areas of your life, but especially sex. When we communicate, it eliminates the practice of mind reading. It allows you and your spouse to clearly define yourself and to know the message has been received. When you communicate your sexual needs, one of three responses can be expected: "yes," "not now," or "no." I realize that these answers can come both by words and/or facial expression. But the most important thing you can do is to be prepared for them. "Yes" is very easy to prepare for. However, without communicating to your spouse your needs, "yes" may not come as often as you would like. "Not now" can be a challenge at times. It may be important to understand why "yes" is not an option at the present time and to ask for clarity from your partner on when "yes" will happen. If you are the spouse setting the time table for sex, being as specific as possible will help him or her handle a less than "yes" answer. Let me also say if one person in the relationship is always deciding when and if sex happens it can create an imbalance in power that can easily lead to feelings of bitterness and resentment. "No" is the last response I would like to discuss. This is not an answer we want to get into a habit of using. Regardless of mood or situation, the answer "no" should be used cautiously. When "no" is warranted, further explanation is always recommended. It may also be helpful to come up with alternatives to the needs expressed by your mate. I will let your imagination take it from here. 1 Corinthians 7:5 (NAS) says, "Stop depriving one another, except by agreement for a time," this verse is not directed at one specific spouse, but should be further testimony of God's desire that we should always seek to serve one another.

Prayer

Satan will use everything possible to attack your marriage, including and especially sex. Intimacy is too important to a relationship not to pray over. When we pray, we take our requests and desires to a higher power. God created sex, and I believe he wants it to be a wonderful part of any marriage. To ask him to bless the union between you and your wife is both appropriate and necessary. Many obstacles are working against a husband and wife when it comes to sex. Whether you are battling young children, a busy work schedule, family or finance issues, emotional distance, sickness, or all the above, life in general is working against a healthy and enjoyable sex life with your spouse. I can think of no better ally to involve in your battle than God. Wives, pray for your husband's patience and sensitivity. Pray that God will give him self-control and an understanding heart. Pray that you will be able to communicate honestly and compassionately your heart. Pray that God will allow you to understand your husband in such a way that you will desire to please him and in doing so please God. Husbands, pray that your wife will have understanding and patience as well and that you will have the ability to listen to her heart. Pray that she will see and know your heart. Pray for the capability to meet her emotional needs and to put her first in your life. Pray that God will create meaningful opportunities for both of you to meet the needs of the other. Pray that sex will be great for both of you. Studies have shown that prayer improves marriage. When we pray for our partner it has been shown to increase forgiveness and gratitude, decrease infidelity and alcohol consumption, and generally cause a couple to better regulate their emotions within the relationship. Statistics support that consistent prayer is associated with greater happiness and less divorce consideration in couples. So pray.

One of the most common questions I receive from Christian couples is how to pray as a couple. To be honest, Heather and I have been working on this for years. Throughout our marriage we have prayed many times together; however, something always gets in the way of consistency. This doesn't surprise me, as I am sure Satan has read the statistics on prayer as well. I think the first thing to do is to get comfortable with praying together. This may come at a specific time of difficulty, during a meal, or before bedtime. It takes very little to say a quick prayer with your spouse. When kids become a part of your family, they will see this activity and know that God is a part of your family and relationship. More times than I can count I have had the opportunity to pray for Heather over the phone. She would call distressed or frustrated, and I would have no answers. A simple prayer for her over the phone allowed me to help at a time when I had no other answers. This action also creates a stronger emotional bond between us as we call God into our relationship.

Secondly, make prayer a habit, not just a lifeline to God when things go wrong. This is where Heather and I sometimes fail. We intend to pray each night together, but somehow, someway, something comes up that takes our time or energy. We know deep down in our hearts that it is right and necessary for both our marriage and for our family. We have currently started praying every Sunday night—so far so good. The key for us is to make it a priority and a habit, not unlike anything else. If is important, it will get done.

In summary, a healthy sex life does not just happen. It takes effort and attention. God desires this to be a positive and rewarding part of your marriage, but it will first take each spouse's ability to see the sacrifice and commitment within the act. Your ability and desire to safely communicate and meet the sexual needs of your partner is the difference between a good sex life and a great one. Finally, don't forget to involve God in your plans. He wants to give you the desires of your heart (Psalms 37:4), so let Him.

Couple Application

1. Make a list of three things you enjoy most about intimacy with your partner. Discuss these items together.

2. Together discuss the intimacy needs that exist for both you and your spouse. Talk about ways to accommodate each other.

Divorce and Blended Families

In today's world, divorce and blended families are very real probabilities. In 2011 over 30 million stepparents[2] in America recognized the unique and challenging obstacles that are created by being a blended family. Divorce is a very difficult thing; there are no two ways about it. When two people marry, separating does not—will not—come without some degree of pain and discomfort for both parties, regardless of the situation. The experience becomes even more trying when you add children into the equation. Divorce is never a good alternative, and I don't believe it ever will be, but it does happen. Over time I have come to recognize that divorce is a product of two people with the inability to reconcile, not necessarily the lack of desire. There are times when hard hearts (Matthew 19:8, NIV) will prevail and no amount of counseling or soul searching appears able to help. Please know that I believe all relationships can be helped and that every marriage, no matter how challenging, has hope. Yes, God hates divorce (Malachi 3, NIV) and permits it only under immorality (Matthew 19:9). But divorce is a very real fact in the world today and thus should be addressed. There *is* life after divorce.

I am a product of divorce. My parents divorced when my brother was six and I was eight. My mother remarried and would later have two children, a son and a daughter, with my stepfather. My stepfather had been married prior and had two children as well, a son and a daughter. My biological father remarried multiple times and had four children, one son and three daughters, following the divorce from my mother. For those of you counting at home, this would leave me with one biological brother, two half-brothers, four half-sisters, a stepbrother and a stepsister, not to mention a very confusing family tree. Growing up, this was not what I had planned for my life, nor had my parents. As with all children of divorce, I felt out of sorts. It was as if someone took from me any opportunity for a normal life. You seldom think about why your parents are divorcing or the good that can come from it. All you think is how messed up life has now become. But this too shall pass. Through my parents' divorce, God was able to show me His perfect plan and a wonderful ability to turn something meant for hurt and pain into something that offered instead hope and encouragement. I am a marriage and family therapist because of my parents' divorce. I can't tell you that life always made sense, but I can tell you that the man, husband, father, and friend I am today is in large part a result of the failure of my parent's marriage. To God be the glory.

A Beginning Not an End

Regardless of the statistics, divorce will never be normal for anyone. Human beings are driven to relationships. It is in our DNA. To break off a relationship is to fail. I don't believe anyone gets married with the goal of someday divorcing. Don't miss the fact that people seldom marry once, that and the amazing growth of online dating, helps illustrate the desire we all have to share life with someone special. When this is disrupted things get chaotic.

Life after a divorce will never be normal for either party, which is why it is important to embrace a *new normal*. Divorce brings about change. Change is not always good or bad; it is often just change. The first year after a divorce is the most difficult, however it is also a time to establish a new normal or the next stage of your life. Within a year of my parents' separation and ultimate divorce, my mom, brother, and I moved back to Oklahoma from California. In practice, I would seldom recommend this type of change for two young boys this soon after a divorce. However, my mother's need to return home to her family, and the support necessary to raise two very active boys was more of a priority than our adjustment. *Key point*: the first priority in any marriage or separation is the wellness of the parents. Children need their parents, and if the parents are less than 100 percent, so too will be the children. If you have ever been on an airplane, you probably remember the flight attendant telling you that in the event of a breach in cabin pressure secure your mask before securing the mask of your children. This is obviously due to the fact that you will be little good to your child passed out on the floor of the plane. My mother's oxygen mask at the time was in Oklahoma. In other words, with our family, the new normal was living in Oklahoma while my father stayed in California. Was this ideal? No. However, we adjusted and through the dedication and commitment of both my mother and father, I was able to maintain a strong and growing relationship with both parents to this very day.

Marriage within the Blended Family

In any family the marriage must be the most important relationship. This is even more critical in a blended family. When your marriage becomes second to your children, conflict will arise. Children know when parents are divided, trust me, and they will use this division to benefit their cause, whatever it may be. I see this in my own family. If either of my kids thinks they can get a yes from one parent and not the other, whom do you think they are going to go to? But show them unity and the ability to talk as a couple before making decisions, and they will recognize the need for honest and upfront communication. However, the most important thing about you and your spouse placing your marriage above anything else is the model you are exhibiting to your children. When your son or daughter becomes a parent, don't you want them to be seen by their spouse as the number one priority in the family? Don't you want them to have this expectation when looking for that special someone to marry? The priority they place on marriage and on how they expect their future partner to treat them comes directly from observing you. And if you are divorced the same holds true. If you are a wife and you treat your ex-husband with distain, your son will see this as normal and might find that he is comfortable being treated the same by his future wife. If you are a husband that talks negatively about your ex-wife, expect your daughter to see this action as acceptable from her future husband as well. Get the picture? Your kids are sponges. The husband and wife they will be someday is directly related to the model you provide, husband to wife, wife to second husband, husband to second wife, it does not matter. What matters is that you *are* having an influence.

Unity as a couple is critical. Regardless of your family's break down, a husband and wife should be unified. Even when you disagree, the rest of the family should see unconditional support and unity within the parental structure. Let me clarify this. In a blended family system you routinely have the parents, the children, and the ex-spouses. All three have an impact, good, bad, or indifferent. But in any blended family, the marriage or parental system must be number one. This means discussing all decisions, understanding all outside relationships, and managing the family as a team. Surprises or differing roles very often lead to bitterness, frustration, and division. When my mother remarried, it was a shock to me and my brother, to say the least. My stepfather was ex army, and you might have easily mistaken him for a drill sergeant. He wasted little time in trying to instill discipline into me and my brother. This would lead to a great deal of conflict in our family as my brother and I became bitter and resentful toward him. You would often find my mom struggling in the middle, loving her boys, but also loyal to her new husband. I would not recommend the aggressive approach of my stepfather to most blended family systems, at least not early on. I believe in hindsight it was his commitment to God and God's Word that made the biggest difference. However, it was also a wonderful picture of marriage to see the commitment my mother had to him and the commitment he also had to my mother, regardless of the conflict. There was little question to their unconditional support and love for each other. I would later take this with me to my own marriage. As I matured, I also gained a new appreciation and respect for my stepfather. His love, commitment, and passion for God, and our family were always evident. Today he is one of my best friends, and I am thankful for the influence he had in my life, even when I didn't think it was needed. Thank you, Larry.

Co-parenting

Parenting is never easy, but add a divorce, and you have something that can seem next to impossible. What is critical to remember is that this is not the end but the beginning. It was just this past summer that I had the opportunity of attending my niece Haylee's wedding in Branson, MO. Haylee's parents have been divorced for many years, but they still were responsible for working together to make this a special moment for their daughter. When divorce occurs within a family, you and your ex-spouse are starting the process of establishing a new normal. This will not always be an easy time, however it can be one of hope and opportunity, but only if both spouses keep the end in mind. The end I am referring to is that of your child or children becoming parents themselves. To co-parent your children with your ex is to continue your role as the parent for the good of the child. It does children little good to play the role of pawn between two feuding parents. The one that will be damaged the most will be the child. Children have a wonderful ability to adjust to divorce, but only when conflict is at a minimum. Numerous studies report that one of the key indicators of a child's development after a divorce is that of the condition of the relationship between the divorcing parents. When extreme conflict exists, so too does a higher probability of problems for the child later in life, including but not limited to: depression, anxiety, academic difficulties, acting out, etc. When ex-spouses put the priority on the children, they directly secure the opportunity for proper adjustment and continued growth within the child.

When you were growing up you collected memories of times throughout your life that made an impression. Today your children are collecting the same memories, regardless of the circumstance. Your job is to assist them with memories that will benefit them as they grow into adulthood, regardless of the impact divorce will play. I remember the day my father said good-bye to our family. I was on the top bunk as he woke us up for school. I remember him telling us that he loved us. Later that morning my mother gave us the news that my parents were getting a divorce. I don't remember what I felt that day, but I do remember a constant concern for my mother. You will find that a child's reaction to divorce is strongly correlated to the condition of one or both of the parents. My relationship with my mother was never in doubt, but some might question the future of my relationship with my dad. Regardless of my mother's emotional struggles during this time and my dad's desire to divorce, I never questioned my dad's love. I remember him taking me for a walk in the park later that week to talk about how I was handling the news. My dad's ability to be available allowed for security in an eight-year-old boy. Even today I believe my relationship with my dad is largely due to his constant availability and commitment. My security was not a product of two parents staying together but more of a result of two loving and committed co-parents. Whether you are across the country or across the street, your ability to be a parent after divorce is correlated to your ability to be emotionally available to your children at all times. This is security for a young child. Divorce will not come without hurt and pain for everyone in the family, but this will pass, and what is left is the relationship.

Parenting With the End in Mind

As parents, it is important to always have the end in mind. You are raising a future husband, wife, mother or father, and your ability to prepare them is the difference maker. Each of us as adults was shaped by our parents. Some have negative memories, some positive, and still some a combination of the two. What matters most is to understand the influence. I was impacted by my parents' divorce in a way that led me to the field of therapy. The statistics are clear: children of divorce are more likely to divorce as adults than children not experiencing divorce. However, the influence is also conditioned on the child. I decided to use my parents' mistakes to better my own ability to succeed. We all have a choice—a choice to impact our children in a more positive way, learning from our parents' mistakes, and growing from our own. I recall not long ago having a bad day one Sunday afternoon and feeling like each member of our family was taking the brunt of it. I decided to have Bible study that evening with the family at the kitchen table. I felt so convicted and wanted to use this as a teaching moment for me and my family. I read John 13, where Christ washed the disciple's feet in the upper room. Can you imagine, the Son of God washing the filthy feet of each of His disciples? What an amazing picture of humility and sacrifice. Embarrassingly, my children don't always see a humble and sacrificial father. I mistakenly think I need to always be strong—to be the leader. However, this was an awesome opportunity to show my wife and kids someone else. As we met as a family that night, I took a bucket of water and towel and washed the feet of my wife, daughter, and son, telling them as I went along, that a dad must be strong, but also humble and a servant. My hopes and prayers that night were that this action would affect the man my son would someday be, the husband my daughter would someday find, and the spouse my wife continued to love. Each and every day we have the opportunity to prepare our children for adulthood—make the most of each moment.

Couple Application (Blended Couples)

1. Plan a date with each one of your step children. Spend one on one time growing the relationship.

2. Plan a family activity the next time you are together. Make sure everyone is participating.

Endnotes:

1   http://blogs.computerworld.com/online_
    dating_its_bigger_than_porn

2   http://www.smartstepfamilies.com/view/
    statistics